CHILDREN OF POVERTY

Studies on the Effects
of Single Parenthood,
the Feminization of Poverty,
and Homelessness

edited by

STUART BRUCHEY
University of Maine

A GARLAND SERIES

HOW THE FAMILY INFLUENCES CHILDREN'S ACADEMIC ACHIEVEMENT

SHUI FONG LAM

GARLAND PUBLISHING, Inc.
NEW YORK & LONDON / 1997

Library of Congress Cataloging-in-Publication Data

Lam, Shui Fong, 1959–
How the family influences children's academic achievement /
Shui Fong Lam.
p.   cm. — (Children of Poverty)
Includes bibliographical references and index.
ISBN 0-8153-2620-3 (alk. paper)
1. Home and school—United States. 2. Education—Parent
participation—United States. 3. Academic achievement—United
States. 4. Students—United States—Social conditions. 5. Family—
United States. I. Title. II. Series.
LC225.3L35 1997   96-39982

Printed on acid-free, 250-year-life paper
Manufactured in the United States of America

Contents

Tables

Figures

Preface

How the family influences children is an intriguing question that has attracted the attention of many researchers. Few researchers would dispute the notion that children are somehow shaped by their families. However, they might have different opinions on how the family affects children. While some researchers focus on the effects of family status, others emphasize the importance of family process.

Family status refers to the conditions of families, such as family structure, ethnic background, socioeconomic status, and family size. Researchers who focus on the effects of family status typically adopt a social address paradigm in research. Social address is an environmental label indicating the ecological niches in which a child lives. In the field of family research, family status is a social address that indicates where a child grows up (e.g. in a single-parent family or low-income family). Using the social address paradigm, researchers typically compare the developmental outcomes of children from families with different statuses. The social address paradigm is a primitive but popular paradigm in the field of family research. However, the social address paradigm does not give consideration to the intervening processes or mechanism through which the family status might affect a child.

In view of the limitations of the social address paradigm, many researchers argue for a shift from the study of family status to family process. Family process refers to behavior or interaction with family members, such as parenting styles, parental discipline and parental involvement in education. Using the family process paradigm, researchers focus on the effects of various family processes on the child's development. However, family status and family process are seldom independent. There is a need to incorporate both sets of family factors in family research. Instead of viewing family status and process as polarized influences, it may be more fruitful to integrate the two paradigms.

In this book, I use an integrated paradigm to study the interactive effects of family status and process on children's academic achievement. The utility of the three research paradigms is demonstrated in a study of a group of students in two inner-city schools. The information presented illustrates the interactive effects of authoritative parenting style, family structure, and socio-economic status on the academic performance of the children. An appreciation of the intricate linkage between family status and process can enhance our understanding of family influences on children. This understanding is important to parents, educators and policy makers as they strive to improve children's well-being.

Acknowledgments

I would like to thank Dr. Sandra Christenson, my advisor at the University of Minnesota, for her contribution to the completion of the study reported in this book. I am thankful for her advice and encouragement. I am also thankful to Mr. Michael Galligan, Editorial Assistant at Garland Publisher, for his support and patience. Last but not least, I would like to convey my deepest gratitude to my sister, Kit-ling, and my brother-in-law, Denis, for their unfailing support and encouragement throughout the writing process. I am particularly indebted to Denis, who has spent many hours editing my manuscript.

How the Family Influences
Children's Academic Achievement

I

Introduction

Children's academic achievement has been shown to be influenced by many family factors (Christenson, Rounds, & Gorney, 1992). In this book, three research paradigms are used to examine the influences of family factors on children's academic achievement. The family factors examined in this books are family structure, socioeconomic status, and parenting styles.

Single-parent households have become a common phenomenon in contemporary America. Statistics indicate that half of American couples married after 1970 will subsequently divorce (Hetherington, 1992). Recent United States Census Bureau figures indicate that nearly one-fourth of children under 18 live with only one parent, usually their mother. There are approximately 6 million single-mother families with children under 18 in the United States (Walters, 1988). Given the fact that family structure in the United States is no longer simple and homogeneous, there is an obvious need for educators to understand the diversity of family structures and its impact on children's academic performance.

Following a divorce, single-mother families typically descend into poverty. According to the 1990 Census Bureau Report, 37.2% of single-parent families were living below the poverty line compared with 12% of all families with children.

The association between socioeconomic background and children's academic achievement perennially attracts attention from many researchers (White, 1982). In view of the changes in family structure and socioeconomic background of American children, researchers need to look at the effects of socioeconomic factors on children's academic achievement in a new light; the interactive effects of family structure have to be taken into consideration.

How parental behavior affects children has also been a popular topic for investigation. There is a well established association between parenting styles and children's academic achievement (Baumrind, 1967; Dornbusch, Ritter, Leiderman, Roberts, & Fraleigh, 1987; Grolnick, & Ryan, 1989; Lamborn, Mounts, Steinberg, & Dornbusch, 1991; Steinberg, Mounts, Lamborn, & Dornbusch, 1991). In contrast to family structure and socioeconomic status, parenting styles are viewed as a process variable instead of as a status variable of a family. The combination of family process and status variables in the study of children's academic achievement reflects a new conceptualization in research methodology. The advantages of this endeavor are evident from a review of research paradigms that have been employed to study child development-in-context.

RESEARCH PARADIGMS

Social Address Paradigm

The social address paradigm is the first and most primitive paradigm employed in investigating child development-in-context (Bronfenbrenner & Crouter, 1983). In the field of family research, the concept of family status is similar to that of social address. Family status refers to the conditions of families, such as family structure, ethnic background, socioeconomic status (SES), parent educational level and family size. Similarly, social address or family status is an environmental label indicating the ecological niches in which a child lives (e.g., in a single-parent household or low-income household). Using the social address paradigm, researchers typically compare the academic performance of children living at different social addresses or in different ecological niches. As Bronfenbrenner and Crouter (1983) point out, the social address paradigm has a serious limitation: no explicit consideration is given to intervening processes through which the social address or environment might affect the development of children. Studying the effects of family structure or socioeconomic background on children's academic achievement often tells us little about the mechanisms by which these different factors might affect academic performance.

Family Process Paradigm

Using the social address paradigm, researchers reliably find unambiguous differences in academic achievement among students from different family structures and socioeconomic backgrounds (e.g. Featherstone, Cundick & Jensen, 1992; Eagle, 1989). However, the strong association between these family characteristics and children's achievement are considerably reduced when achievement-related family processes are taken into consideration. The British Psychological Society reported that "Material circumstances and class position seem less important than what may be referred to as family 'climate,' which includes parents' aspirations and attitudes and the support and encouragement for their child's schooling" (British Psychological Society, 1986, p.124).

In view of the weaknesses of the social address paradigm and the powerful impact of family processes, Dornbusch and Wood (1989) argue for a shift from the study of social address to the study of family process. They argue that if we focus on family status such as family structure, parent educational level, ethnicity, and socioeconomic status, we may be "selling short the majority of our children when we assume incorrectly that acquired and irrevocable intellectual advantages and disadvantages fall within lines demarcated by class, ethnicity, and household structure" (1989, p.67). Dornbusch and Wood argue that family processes are more important than family status. They defines family processes as behaviors and interactions with family members such as parenting styles, parental discipline and parental involvement in education. They suggest that more work is needed to identify specific family processes that produce differences in educational achievement. They further argue that if such processes are identified, the findings might suggest alternative ways of relating to children that will foster academic achievement. They believe that such a search is for universal and the generaliztions are "not limited to an ethnic group, a period, or a community" (1989, p.68).

A Synthesis of Two Research Paradigms

By setting aside family status and focusing on universal family processes, Dornbusch and Wood (1989) have provided significant insight into the dynamic relationships between environmental factors and student academic achievement.

However, family status and family processes are seldom independent factors. Instead of viewing family status and processes as polarized influences, it may be more fruitful to integrate the two perspectives. As early as 1975, Halsey (1975) pointed out that in much family research, the concept of social status "is trivialized to the point where differences of parental attitude are conceived of as separate factors rather than an integral part of the work and community situation of children" (1975, p.17). Later Kohn (1979) argued that the values and child-rearing practices of American parents must be seen in terms of the realities parents face. The effects of family processes on educational experience are usually not independent of the effects of family status. This perspective is supported by many studies reviewed in Chapter II below.

Milne (1989) argues that neither family status nor process variables should be omitted from future research models. Because of the interactive effects of family status and family processes on children's academic achievement, I agree with Milne that we should incorporate both sets of variables in our research. Instead of switching entirely from a social address paradigm to a family process paradigm, we need to integrate the two when studying the effects of family factors on children's academic achievement.

Family Processes as Mediators

Our knowledge of family environment and student achievement would be considerably enhanced if we could distinguish the direct effects from the indirect effects (through family processes) of family status on student achievement.

Baron and Kenny (1986) point out that the functions of moderator and mediator variables are often confused in research in social science. A moderator "partitions a focal independent variable into subgroups that establish its domains of maximal effectiveness in regard to a given dependent variable" (p.1173). For example, Steinberg et al. (1991) used SES, family structure and ethnicity to partition their 10,000 high school students into 16 subgroups. The impact of authoritative parenting was examined in each of the subgroups. The authors found authoritative parenting to be associated with better children's academic achievement across all subgroups. In other words, SES, family structure and ethnicity did not moderate the influence of authoritative parenting on students' achievement. In contrast to moderating influences, a mediator "represents the generative mechanism through which the focal independent variable is able to influence the dependent variable of interest" (Baron & Kenny, 1986, p.1173). For example, Milne , Myers, and Ginsburg (1986) used parental expectations, other family processes, and SES as mediators to explain the effects of family structure on student achievement. They found that the effects of family structure on children's academic achievement were reduced significantly when these mediators were taken into consideration.

Given the fact that there are joint and interactive effects of family status and processes, there is an obvious need to disentangle the direct and indirect effects of family status on children's academic achievement. In other words, there is a need to investigate how much of the effect of family status on children's academic achievement is mediated by family processes. We need to shift from exclusively using family status as moderating variables to incorporating family processes as mediating variables. Instead of asking if family status moderates family processes, we need to ask the following questions: (a) What are the mediating effects of a specific family process on the influences of family status on children's academic achievement? (b) What are the direct effects of a specific family status on children's academic achievement? (c) What are the indirect effects of a specific family status through a specific family processes on children's academic achievement?

RESEARCH QUESTIONS

In the present investigation, I examine the effects of the family on children's academic achievement with each of the three research paradigms. I examine family influences first with a social address paradigm and then with a family process paradigm. Finally an integrated paradigm which incorporates both social address and family process paradigms will be employed. Both family status and process variables will be included. The family status variables used in the present investigation are family structure and socioeconomic status. I am particularly interested in the comparison between intact families and single-mother families. The family process variables include three dimensions of authoritative parenting style: (1) parental monitoring/supervision; (2) parental supportiveness/warmth; and (3) psychological autonomy (Steinberg, 1990). These three dimensions are incorporated as mediating variables in the present study (see Figure 1).

Figure 1 is a model in which parental monitoring, parental supportiveness and psychological autonomy-granting mediate the effects of socioeconomic status and family structure on children's academic achievement.

There are two specific purposes of this book:

(1) To examine the relationships of socioeconomic status, family structure, authoritative parenting style and children's

academic achievement envisioned by each of the three research paradigms: the social address paradigm, the family process paradigm, and the integrated paradigm.

(2) To compare the effectiveness of the three paradigms in explaining how families influence the academic achievement of children.

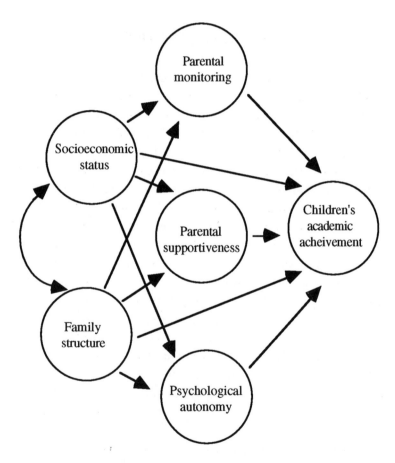

Figure 1. Model incorporating both status and process variables in studying family effects on student academic achievement.

II

Family Factors and Academic Achievement

This chapter provides a review of the literature on the influences of the family on children's academic achievement. It consists of three sections: (1) family structure and children's academic achievement; (2) socioeconomic status and children's academic achievement; and (3) parenting styles and children's academic achievement. Throughout the three sections, emphasis is placed on the interactive effects of family status and process variables on children's achievement, as well as on the evaluation of research methodologies.

FAMILY STRUCTURE AND CHILDREN'S ACADEMIC ACHIEVEMENT

The Social Address Paradigm and Family Structure

Bronfenbrenner and Crouter (1983) point out that the social address paradigm is a century-old paradigm that continues to characterize the majority of present day investigations. Their observation is particularly true in regards to the study of children from single-parent families. Ambert and Saucier's study (1984) on children from intact vs. non-intact families is a representative example of studies based on the social address paradigm. These investigators surveyed a large sample of Montreal teenagers and found that adolescents from separated/divorced families did less well in school, liked school less, and expected to abandon school earlier than adolescents from intact families. However, since they did not control for socioeconomic or ethnic factors, it is not known if the results were influenced by these factors or were due solely to family structure, as the authors implied.

Studies based on the social address paradigm vary considerably in their sophistication in controlling confounding variables. The most common form of statistical control in the literature is to have social class, race, grade level, or age controlled. A recent study by Featherstone, Cundick & Jensen (1992) on 530 students is representative of such studies. They compared school behavior and achievement among students from intact, reconstituted, and single-parent families. With race, grade and age included as covariates in the analysis, they found that students from intact two-parent families had better attendance, higher grade point averages, and fewer negative and more positive behavioral ratings by their teachers than children from reconstituted and single-parent families. However, their study did not deal with the distinctive confounding variable of socioeconomic status.

SES as a Confounding Variable

Family structure and socioeconomic status are closely related. The median income of single-mother households is one-third that of two-parent households. One-fourth of white single-parent families and nearly one-half of black single-parent families lives in poverty (Walters, 1988). In their classic review of the effects of father absence on juvenile delinquency, academic achievement, and adjustment, Herzog and Sudia (1973) emphasized the importance of controlling for SES in research dealing with the effects of father absence. They emphasized this importance by restricting their review to studies with a control or comparison group that was in some way matched for SES and cultural background. With this restriction, they found that father absence in itself had a lower correlation with poor school achievement if SES and type of fatherlessness were adequately controlled (Herzog and Sudia, 1973).

A study by Mueller and Cooper (1986) extended the effects of family structure beyond children's academic achievement. They employed a control group to study the effect of family structure on social adjustment in early adulthood. Their subjects were 1,448 young adults in the U.S. Midwest. They found that the lower educational attainment of respondents reared in single-parent families appeared to be the result of the economic disadvantage of such families rather than their structure. However, for some other outcomes, such as economic attainment and marital stability, children from single-parent families fared less well than their counterparts from two-parent families, even after the economic conditions of the family of origin were controlled.

Mueller and Cooper's study (1986) was partially supported by that of Acock and Kiecolt (1989) who used data from the 1972-1986 *General Social Surveys* to investigate the long-term effects of family structure during adolescence on adult adjustment. When SES was not controlled, both men and women who lived in intact families at age 16 scored significantly higher than those from single-parent families on all aspects of adjustment. However, when SES during adolescence was controlled, a few adverse effects of parental divorce, but no effects of a father's death were observed.

Subtypes of Single-Parent Families and Children's Achievement

There is a need to consider subtypes of single-parent families in children's achievement research because single-parent families are obviously not a homogeneous group. The study by Zimiles and Lee (1991) exemplifies such an attempt. They compared children from three different types of families (intact, single-parent, and step families) with respect to high school grades and educational persistence. Based on a large sample (N = 13,532) from a national data set (*High School and Beyond Study*), they found that differences among the three groups with regard to achievement test scores and high school grades were slight but statistically significant. Children from both single-parent and step families lagged behind those from intact families but were indistinguishable from each other. This trend persisted even after SES was taken into account.

Larger group differences were found in educational persistence and drop-out behavior in Zimiles and Lees' (1991) study. Students from single-parent and step families were almost three times as likely to leave high school before graduation as those from intact families. This trend persisted even after SES and ability differences were taken into account. Interestingly, striking gender differences were found in drop-out behavior. Adolescents who lived in single-parent families were more likely to drop out when they had an unlike-gender custodial parent. A similar pattern of interaction was found among step families, but the pattern was reversed. Adolescents who lived with their same gender custodial parent were more prone to drop out.

Family Structure and Family Processes

As previously noted, studies such as that of Zimiles and Lee (1991), enhance our knowledge of the effects of family structure on children, but give us no understanding of the processes or mechanisms responsible in different environments for the academic performance of children. Milne et al. (1986) attempted to include processes in the study of the educational achievement of children from single-parent families. Working with two national data bases (*Sustaining Effects Study of Title,* N = 12,429 and *High School and Beyond,* N = 2,720), Milne and her colleagues examined the effects of living in a one-parent family on children's academic achievement. In their analysis, they not only examined the effects of SES, race, and age, but also the effects of several process variables including their custodial mother's educational expectations, number of books in the home, homework monitoring, and time use at home. They found that children from two-parent families had higher scores on reading and math achievement tests than children from one-parent families. This trend persisted even after race and age were taken into account. However, they found that the effects of family structure were almost entirely mediated by other variables, particularly by income. With this factor isolated, the direct effects of family structure were much smaller (about one-third the size of the total effects). They also found that parents' educational expectations for children were significant mediators of the effect of family structure. Based on the small and nonsignificant direct effects of family structure on academic achievement, Milne et al. (1986) argued that the negative effects of living in a one-parent family work primarily through other variables, such as SES and parents' educational expectation.

Somewhat surprisingly, Milne et al. (1986) did not find significant mediating effects of the other processes they examined, such as homework monitoring and time use at home on the relation between family structure and academic achievement. Their results were partially replicated in a subsequent study by Astone and McLanahan (1991). Using data from the *High School and Beyond study*, they found that children who lived with single parents or step parents during adolescence received less encouragement and less help with school work than children who lived with both natural parents. They also found that parental involvement had positive effects on children's school achievement. However, differences in these family processes accounted for little of the difference in educational attainment between children from intact and non-intact families. Family structure effects were reduced by no more than 15 percent when these family processes were controlled. The failure to find mediating effects of family processes may be due to the limitation of large scale surveys which cannot accurately capture significant details of complex information on family processes.

More detailed studies of family processes substantiate this statement. For example, Blum, Boyle, and Offord (1988) interviewed 1,869 families in Canada and found that children of single-parent families were more at risk for child psychiatric disorders and poor school performance. However, when variables indicative of economic hardship and family dysfunction were controlled, the relationships between single-parent family status and childhood psychiatric disorder and poor school performance became statistically nonsignificant. These findings are concordant with those of Amato and Keith

(1991) who performed a meta-analysis on 92 studies of parental divorce and the well-being of children. They found that children of divorced families scored lower than children in intact families across a variety of outcomes. However, they also found that children from divorced families appeared to have a higher level of well-being than children in high-conflict families. The results of their meta-analysis show that family conflict strongly influences the relation between family structure and the well-being of children.

Family dysfunction or conflict is not the only family process that has attracted the attention of researchers. The parenting styles and specific childrearing behaviors of single parents is another area of current interest. Health and MacKinnon (1988) studied factors related to the social competence of children in 80 single-parent families. They found that the childrearing behavior of single parents was an important factor in their children's social competence. Single mothers were found to be lax in control more often with their sons than with their daughters. Firm control was shown to be a more important predictor of high social competence levels for sons whereas moderate control was predictive of high social competence scores for daughters.

The finding that single mothers are lax in control more often with sons than with daughters partially replicates the findings of Dornbusch, Carlsmith, Bushwall, Ritter, Leiderman, Hastorf, and Gross (1985). These investigators used a representative national sample of adolescents (N = 7,514) to examine the interrelationships among family structure, patterns of family decision making, and deviant behavior among adolescents. Their results showed that adolescents in single-parent families were more likely to make decisions without direct parental input and more likely to exhibit deviant behavior than children from intact families.

The findings of Amato (1987) on 342 students corroborate those of Health and MacKinnon (1988) and Dornbusch, et al.(1985). He found that adolescents in one-parent families reported that their mothers exercised a relatively low level of control. In addition, adolescents in one-parent families reported significantly higher autonomy (number of decisions made by adolescents themselves) when compared with adolescents in other family types. Amato identified several family processes in different family structures, but he did not try to relate these processes to the well-being of the children. Collectively these studies emphasize that there is a continuing need to explore how family processes such as parenting styles mediate the effects of family structure on the well-being of children.

SOCIOECONOMIC STATUS AND CHILDREN'S ACHIEVEMENT

The Impact of Socioeconomic Status

There is a well established association between socioeconomic background and children's achievement. As early as the 1960s, Coleman and his colleagues (1966) in their famous *Equality of Educational Opportunity Survey* concluded that "schools bring little influence to bear on a child's achievement that is independent of his background and general social context" (Coleman, Campbell, Hobson, McPartland, Mood, Weinfeld, & York, 1966, p.325). Many studies conducted in the following decades confirmed these general findings (Balua & Duncan, 1967; Flanangan, Shanycroft, Richards, & Claudy, 1971; Bowles, 1977; Eagle, 1989).

Blau and Duncan (1967) found that the educational level and occupation of the father accounted for 28% of the variance in years of schooling in a sample of more than 20,000 males between the ages of 20 and 64. Flanangan et al. (1971) also found that the probability of a student from the lower SES quartile entering college within five years of high school graduation was .32 for males and .18 for females, while the probability for students from the highest quartile was .86 for males and .78 for females. Bowles (1977) pointed out that children from the 90th percentile in social class distribution (social class being defined by the income, occupation, and educational level of the parents) may be expected to receive over four and a half more years of schooling than children from the 10th percentile. In a more recent study, Eagle (1989) examined data from the National Center for Education Statistics, and once again confirmed the association between socioeconomic status and educational attainment. In her study, about 45% of high school seniors from high SES backgrounds completed postsecondary education while only 15% of high school seniors from low SES backgrounds did so.

When scores on scholastic tests rather than college entrance are taken as the outcome measure, SES appears to account for somewhat less of the variance. Marjoribanks (1980) found that parental social background accounted for 6% of the variance on math, slightly more than 16% of the variance on word knowledge, and 13% on word comprehension. In a sample of 868 black and white elementary school children from two-parent and single-mother families, Patterson, Kupersmidt, and Vaden (1990) found that income level and ethnicity were better overall predictors of children's academic achievement than gender or family structure.

Although there is a considerable amount of evidence for an association between SES and academic achievement, some researchers (e.g. White, 1982) challenged the hypothesis that SES determines the educational achievement of children. White (1982) conducted a meta-analysis of 200 studies which examined the relation between SES and academic achievement. He found that when SES was defined by income, education, and/or occupation of household heads, and when individual students were the unit of analysis, SES and academic achievement were only weakly correlated ($r = .22$). However, he also found that when aggregated unit (such as school or district in which all students were given the same SES and achievement rating) instead of individual students was the unit of analysis, the correlation between SES and academic achievement drastically jumped to .73.

Socioeconomic Status and Family Processes

White (1982) pointed out inconsistencies in the various measures of SES used in the studies he reviewed. Among the traditional measures of SES (income, education, and occupation), income was found to be the highest single correlate of academic achievement. He also found that measures of SES that combine two or more indicators were more highly correlated with academic achievement than any single indicator.

Though it is controversial to define SES by family processes, White found that when SES was defined by measures of home atmosphere, such as parents helping children with homework, SES correlated much higher with academic achievement than when SES was defined by any single or combined group of the traditional indicators of SES. White pointed out that in addition to parental education, occupation, and income level, there were many other characteristics of families that could affect the academic achievement of children. He argued that some low-SES parents (defined in terms of income, education, and/or occupational level) could be effective at creating a home atmosphere that fostered learning, whereas other low-SES parents were not.

The findings of Clark's (1983) study in an African American ghetto support White's argument. He found that sponsored independence, high support, high expectations, close supervision, and respect for their child's intellectual achievement characterized poor black parents of high scholastic achievers.

The arguments of White (1982) and the work of Clark (1983) highlight the limitations of the social address paradigm previously discussed. There is a need to go beyond the SES and look into how SES influences family processes and subsequently the academic achievement of children. This does not mean that SES should be ignored. As Halsey (1975) has argued, socioeconomic class should not be thought of as a single factor independent of family processes. There are complicated interactive relations between SES, family processes and children's achievement.

Kohn (1979) was one of the pioneering researchers who investigated the effects of social class on family processes. He concluded that the values and child-rearing practices of American parents must be seen in terms of the realities parents faced. In his study of the effects of social class on parental values, Kohn (1977) found that the higher a parent's social-class position, the more likely he or she was to value characteristics indicative of self-direction and the less likely he or she was to value characteristics indicative of conformity to external authority. Kohn suggested that this pattern was related to the different conditions of life faced by parents in different socioeconomic positions. Parents with high SES were more typically independent, more free from close supervision, more likely worked at non routine tasks, and to do more complex work than parents with low SES. Hence, they were more likely to value characteristics such as independence and self-direction in their children.

While Kohn related SES to parental values, he did not directly relate parental values to specific child developmental outcomes. This omission was remedied by a longitudinal study of how social address influences family processes and subsequently academic achievement. The longitudinal study by Majoribanks (1988) found that parents' aspirations had differential linear and curvilinear associations with the educational and occupational outcomes of young adults from different social-status groups. For young adults in middle social-status families, parental aspirations were not related to their educational attainment, whereas, in lower social-status families, parental aspirations had a curvilinear association with educational attainment until a threshold level of aspirations was attained.

A study by Datcher-Loury (1988) attempted to link SES and family processes with school achievement of children. Based on data from the *ETS-Head Start Longitudinal Study*, she found that parental behavior and attitudes (such as reading to children several times a week, attending PTA or Head Start groups, and having high educational expectations) had important long-term effects on children's academic performance.

However, it is noteworthy that these achievement-related behaviors of parents are usually associated with SES. Eagle (1989) found that among high school seniors, advantageous home environments (defined by a high degree of parental involvement in high school, parents' reading to the student during early childhood, and having a special place in the household for the student to study) were more common in higher than in low SES households. This finding is consistent with that of a qualitative study on family-school relationships by Lareau (1987). She found that social class provided parents with unequal resources to comply with teachers' requests for parental participation. As a result, middle-class parents were more likely to comply with teachers' requests for parental participation. She found that parents from middle-class and working-class had more differences in the ways they promoted educational success than in their educational values. Working-class parents typically surrendered the responsibility for education to teachers, but middle-class parents did not. Moreover, middle-class parents had more "cultural capital" (educational skills, occupational prestige, and the necessary economic resources to manage child care, transportation and time required to meet with teachers) to facilitate compliance with teachers' requests for parental participation.

PARENTING STYLES AND CHILDREN'S ACADEMIC ACHIEVEMENT

Early Conceptualization of Parenting Styles

How parental behaviors affect children has a long history of investigation. Baumrind is one of the noteworthy pioneers in this area. In her early studies (1967, 1971, 1977, 1979), she identified three clusters of parental styles which she defined as authoritative, authoritarian, and permissive parenting. Each parenting style was found to be associated with different child outcomes.

Authoritative parenting contains the following elements: (a) expectation of mature behavior from the child and clear standard setting; (b) firm enforcement of rules and standards; (c) encouragement of the child's independence and individuality; (d) open communication between parents and children; and (e) recognition of the rights of both parents and children. In her studies on preschool and elementary school children, Baumrind found that children of authoritative parents rated higher in social and cognitive competence than children of non-authoritative parents.

The second cluster is authoritarian parenting. Authoritarian parents (a) attempt to shape, control, and evaluate the behavior and attitudes of their children in accordance with an absolute set of standards; (b) value obedience, respect for authority, work, tradition, and preservation of order; and (c) discourage verbal give-and-take between parent and child. Baumrind found that this parenting style was associated with low levels of independence and social responsibility among preschool children.

The third cluster is permissive parenting. Permissive parents have the following characteristics: (a) they are tolerant and accepting toward the child's impulses; (b) they use little punishment; (c) they make few demands for mature behavior; and (d) they allow considerable self-regulation by the child. Baumrind found the preschool children of permissive parents to be immature, lacking in impulse control and self-reliance, and evidencing a lack of social responsibility and independence. In follow-up studies in middle childhood, these children were low in both social and cognitive competence.

Baumrind's early work focused on preschool and elementary school children. In the 1980s, Dornbusch and his colleagues (1987) extended Baumrind's typology of parenting to a large and diverse sample of adolescents. They found that while both authoritarian and permissive parenting styles were negatively associated with grades, authoritative parenting was positively associated with grades. Parenting styles generally showed these consistent relations to grades across gender, age, parental education, ethnic, and family structure categories except in Asian groups.

The characterizing typology of authoritative, authoritarian, and permissive parenting has been extensively applied in research. However, finer distinctions such as that between neglectful-permissive and indulgent-permissive are unclear or typically ignored in this typology. A new method of characterizing parenting styles is needed to remedy these limitations.

Two-dimensional Approach to Parenting Styles

In her recent work (1989, 1991), Baumrind has shifted her focus from the analysis of the three parenting types described above to the analysis of two dimensions of parenting: demandingness and responsiveness. These two dimensions are thought to grasp the underlying differences of parenting types. As illustrated in Figure 2, she used these dimensions to derive a fourfold classification of parenting styles: (a) authoritative, (b) authoritarian, (c) permissive, and a new category, (d) rejecting-neglecting.

According to Baumrind (1991), authoritative parents are both demanding and responsive. They monitor and impart clear standards for their children's conduct. They are assertive, but not intrusive or restrictive. Authoritarian parents, in contrast, are demanding and directive, but not responsive. They provide an orderly environment and a clear set of regulations for their children and monitor them carefully. However, they are obedience-oriented and expect their orders to be obeyed without explanation. Permissive parents are characterized as being more responsive than they are demanding. They are nontraditional and lenient. They do not require mature behavior of their children and allow considerable self-regulation. The rejecting-neglecting parents are neither demanding nor responsive. They neither structure nor monitor their child's behavior. While characteristically nonsupportive, they may reject or neglect their childrearing responsibilities altogether.

Responsiveness

	High	Low
High Demandingness	Authoritative	Authoritarian
Low	Permissive	Rejecting-Neglecting

Figure 2. Baumrind's fourfold classification of parenting styles.

Compared to Baumrind's earlier typology, the fourfold classification of parenting styles can better distinguish parents who are indulgent-permissive and neglectful-permissive. Based on a similar conceptualization of parenting styles, Lamborn, Mounts, Steinberg, and Dornbusch (1991) examined the interactive effects of parental warmth/involvement and strictness/supervision on four sets of high school student outcomes, including psychosocial development, school achievement, internalized distress, and problem behavior. Their results indicated that adolescents who characterized their parents as authoritative scored highest on measures of psychosocial competence and lowest on measures of psychological and behavioral dysfunction. The reverse was true for the adolescents who describe their parents as neglectful.

Adolescents of authoritarian parents scored reasonably well on measures indexing obedience and conformity to the standards of adults but had relatively poorer self-concepts than other youngsters. In contrast, adolescents whose parents were characterized as indulgent had a strong sense of self-confidence but reported a higher frequency of substance abuse and school misconduct and were less committed to academic achievement. On the basis of a similar two-dimensional approach to parenting, Shucksmith, Hendry, and Glenidinning (1995) identified four types of parenting styles (permissive, problem parent-adolescent relationship, authoritative, and authoritarian) in a sample of 2,035 adolescents. The four types of parenting were based on different levels of acceptance and control. Authoritative parenting was characterized by high levels of acceptance and control. It was found to be the best parental style as measured by school integration and the psychological well-being of the adolescents.

The two-dimensional approach can better distinguish parents who are indulgent-permissive and neglectful-permissive. A major problem in the old typology is thus resolved by this two-dimensional approach. However, this new approach is not free of problem. Lewis (1981) found that there are contradictions between studies of firm parental control and attribution theory. Specifically, attribution theory suggests that firm parental control should be kept at a minimum to maximize a child's compliance with norms and the internalization of norms. Lewis argued that the measures of parental control in Baumrind's studies (1967, 1971) may be reinterpreted as measures of the child's willingness to obey or as the absence of parent-child conflict. According to her, a child's willingness to obey depends on whether or not the rules are derived by democratic practices.

The apparent contradiction between Lewis and Baumrind can be reconciled by a close examination of Baumrind's responsiveness dimension. Lewis' emphasis on the importance of democratic processes by which children internalize or fail to internalize rules is reflected in Baumrind's emphasis on psychological autonomy, which she has incorporated into her responsiveness dimension. In her conceptualization, responsiveness includes both affective warmth and cognitive responsiveness. By affective warmth, Baumrind (1989) implies a parent's emotional expressiveness or love. Cognitive responsiveness refers to "intellectual stimulation and to encouragement of the child to express his or her point of view, often in the context of a disciplinary encounter" (Baumrind, 1989, p.366). Baumrind emphasizes that cognitive responsiveness implies verbal reciprocity (i.e. give and take) and negotiation of differences.

Actually, both Baumrind and Lewis realize the importance of psychological autonomy for children. However, when Baumrind combines psychological autonomy and affective warmth into a single dimension of responsiveness, a single score on responsiveness tends to obscure any differences between parents who are high in affective warmth, but low in cognitive responsiveness, and those who have the reversed pattern. The confusion can be avoided by treating affective warmth and psychological autonomy as two separate dimensions.

The Latest Conceptualization of Parenting Style

As suggested above, adding a third dimension of "psychological autonomy" to Baumrind's two-dimensional model is a logical way to resolve confusion and arguments about parental control. Maccoby and Martin (1983) reviewed the literature on parents' child-rearing behaviors and found that factor analyses in some early studies (e.g. Schaefer, 1959; Becker, 1964) identified two operant variables. Schaefer (1959) analyzed the intercorrelations of variables from a number of studies, showing that they can be ordered into two dimensions: (a) warmth/hostility, and (b) control/autonomy. Becker (1964) proposed two similar dimensions: (a) warmth (acceptance) versus hostility (rejection), and (b) restrictive versus permissive. There is little confusion about the dimension of warmth/hostility, but the dimension of restrictiveness has caused much confusion as indicated in the contradiction between Lewis and Baumrind. One of the difficulties stems from the varying perspectives of different investigators on the restrictiveness dimension. Different researchers may choose a different parenting characteristic as the opposite of firm parental control. For example, Becker (1964) identified a permissive style as the opposite of firm parental control. In contrast, Schaefer (1959) specified a democratic style as the opposite of firm parental control (see Figure 3).

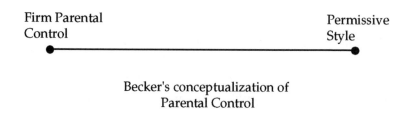

Becker's conceptualization of
Parental Control

Schaefer's conceptualization of
Parental Control

Figure 3. Comparison of Becker's and Schaefer's conceptualization of parental control.

Lewis' (1981) challenge of the role of parental control can be regarded as a logical extension of the argument that parental control is the opposite of psychological autonomy. If psychological autonomy is conceptualized as an independent dimension and if permissiveness is conceptualized as the opposite of parental control, disagreement about the positive effect of parental control can be resolved.

The literature on parental control provides consistent evidence that disruptions or omissions of parental control are associated with antisocial behavior in preadolescents (West & Farrington, 1973, Patterson & Stouthamer-Loeber, 1984, Rutter,

Tizard, & Whitmore, 1970). However, while parental control is an important parental characteristic, high parental control without democratic processes may undermine the internalization of parental rules and social norms by children and consequently decrease its desirability.

Authoritative parenting is multifaceted. Steinberg (1990) suggests that three distinct features characterize this pattern of parenting: (a) a high degree of warmth or acceptance, (b) a high degree of behavioral control, and (c) a high degree of psychological autonomy or democracy. The first two features are well set out in Baumrind's (1989, 1991) two-dimensional approach to parenting. Psychological autonomy which is incorporated as part of the dimension of warmth/acceptance in Baumrind's model, becomes a distinct dimension in Steinberg's model. As a result, there is a clearer distinction between authoritative and authoritarian parenting and much of the confusion and disagreement about parental control can be avoided.

Using a multi-dimensional approach, Steinberg and his colleagues have done a series of studies on authoritative parenting and adolescent adjustment. Steinberg, Elmen, and Mounts (1989) examined school achievement in a sample of 120 10-16 year-old adolescents to test the hypothesis that authoritative parenting conduces to school success. They found that all three components of authoritativeness (i.e. warmth/acceptance, parental control, and psychological autonomy) made independent contributions to school achievement. In another study, Steinberg and his colleagues (1991) found that the positive correlates of authoritative parenting transcended ethnicity, socioeconomic status, and family structure. Regardless of their ethnicity, class, or parents' marital status, adolescents whose parents were perceived as accepting, firm, and democratic earned high grades in school and behaved in socially appropriate ways. This finding replicates studies by Dornbusch, et al. (1987) and Lamborn, et al. (1991), in which family status was not found to moderate the relation between authoritative parenting and child outcome.

Grolnick and Ryan (1989) are another team of researchers who have employed a multi-dimensional model. They identified three dimensions of parenting: (a) autonomy support, (b) structure, and (c) involvement. These dimensions approximate the dimensions of psychological autonomy, firm control and acceptance/involvement in the study of Steinberg et al. (1991). Grolnick and Ryan found that parental autonomy support was positively related to children's self-reports of autonomous self-regulation, teacher-rated competence and adjustment, and school grades and achievement. Maternal involvement was related to achievement, and some aspects of behavioral adjustment, while structure provided by parents was primarily related to children's understanding or knowledge of rules.

Ethnic and Social-class Differences in Parenting Styles

Baumrind (1991) warns that special survival techniques and strategies adopted by ethnic subcultures to cope with their environment and ethnic status should be seriously considered in studying parental behavior. She points out that methods of socialization that by middle-class white standards appear authoritarian, punitive, or seductive may help African-American adolescents to cope with the hazards of contemporary ghetto life. Ethnic and social-class parenting differences are well documented in the literature. Dornbusch, et al. (1987)

found that their typology applied best for white students but least well for Asian American students. Their results were replicated by Lamborn, et al. (1991) and Steinberg, et al., (1991). However, the moderating effects of SES, ethnicity and family structure were not reported. In the study by Steinberg, et al. (1991), 10,000 high school students were grouped into 16 ecological niches defined by ethnicity, SES and family structure. Authoritative parenting was positively associated with school performance in each of the 16 ecological niches.

Methodological Concerns

Sample sizes of subject populations in this research area range from 100 to 10,000. In studies with smaller sample sizes (e.g. Baumrind, 1967, 1971, 1977, 1979, Grolnick & Ryan, 1989, Steinberg, et al., 1989), direct observation, intensive structured interviews, or standardized psychological tests are frequently employed. In contrast, comprehensive data collection employing these intensive methods are rather difficult to carry out in studies with large sample sizes (e.g. Dornbusch, et al., 1987, Lamborn, et al., 1991, Steinberg, et al. 1991). In the latter studies, data are typically collected through questionnaires completed by the adolescent subjects themselves. These studies have an advantage over the small scale studies in that their samples are usually large and diverse. However, the measurements employed may not be as comprehensive, sensitive, or accurate as those used in intensive studies with smaller samples. There is always a trade-off between the quantity and quality of data in psychosocial research.

Since the questionnaires used in most large-sample studies are typically completed by the adolescents themselves, input from parents is rarely included. Though there has been some effort to solicit information from both parents and adolescents (Collins, 1990; Paulson, 1992; Paulson, Hill, & Holmeck, 1991; Smetana, 1988), the parents' and adolescents' perceptions of parenting behaviors may not always be in agreement. For example, Paulson (1992) found that both mothers and fathers reported significantly higher levels of parental demands, responsiveness, and commitment for themselves than their adolescents reported for them. In her study, there was only low to moderate correlation between the adolescents' and their parents' reports. In addition, though the boys' reports of their parents' parenting characteristics significantly correlated with their academic achievement, parents' own reports of their parenting characteristics did not correlate with achievement outcomes in their sons. Because of the intrusion of social desirability into self-report instruments, it is important for researchers to verify their accuracy with other sources of information.

Finally, in some of the large-sample studies, the age range of the subjects was correspondingly large. For example, the subjects in the study by Lamborn et al.(1991) were 14 to 18 years old. Parental strictness is a function of the age of children. Parents may be more controling and have stricter standards for adolescents aged 14 than for adolescents aged 18. Pooling adolescents of different ages into one sample may dilute the influence of parenting styles.

SUMMARY

Evidence that both family status and process variables have interactive and joint effects on children's academic achievement is provided in the literature. For example, while we know that parental involvement is positively associated with children's achievement, Eagle (1989) and Lareau (1987) demonstrated that parental involvement in education is less frequent in families with low SES. Astone and McLanahan (1991) also found that adolescents who lived with single parents or stepparents received less parental involvement with schoolwork than did adolescents who lived with both natural parents. Similarly, while we know that lax parental control is positively associated with poor children outcomes, Dornbusch, et al. (1985) and Amato (1987) showed that single parents tend to exercise a relatively low level of control. These considerations suggest that a synthesis of the social address paradigm and family process paradigm is justified.

The literature also suggests other important issues for consideration in future research. First, different child outcomes have been found among different types of single-parent families (Zimiles and Lee, 1991). Since the dynamics in a step-family are different from those in an intact family, they cannot be grouped into a single category of two-parent families. Similarly, single-mother families and single-father families cannot be grouped into a single category of single-parent families. Second, the magnitude of the association between SES and children's academic achievement depends on the unit of analysis employed and how academic achievement and SES are defined (White, 1982). Measures of SES that combine two or more indicators are more highly correlated with academic achievement than any single indicator. Third, the conceptualization of parenting styles has undergone some major changes in the past three decades. The latest multidimensional approach appears to be quite promising for future research in this area. Fourth, while there have been some studies on the moderating effects of family status variables on the relation between parenting styles and school performance, few studies specifically focus on the mediating effects of parenting styles on the relation between family status variables and school performance. Fifth, as it is difficult to collect comprehensive data from a large sample with intensive methods, trade-offs between quality and quantity of data are manifest throughout the research on parenting styles. All five of these considerations are incorporated into the methodology of the study reported in the following chapters.

HYPOTHESES

The primary purpose of the study presented in this book was to investigate how the family influences children's academic achievement. The relationships of socioeconomic status, family structure, authoritative parenting and children's academic achievement was examined within the framework of the three research paradigms discussed in Chapter I. The results found in each of the three research paradigms was compared to achieve a better understanding of the influences of the family on children's academic achievement. According to the findings of past research and the stipulations of the three research paradigms, the following hypotheses were formulated:

(1) Children from intact families and high SES would have higher academic performance than children from single-mother families and low socioeconomic backgrounds.

(2) Children who reported having more parental monitoring, parental supportiveness, and psychological autonomy would have higher academic performance than those who reported having less parental monitoring, parental supportiveness, and psychological autonomy.

(3) The academic performance of children from single-mother families with high parental monitoring, supportiveness, and psychological autonomy would not differ from that of children from intact families with low parental monitoring, supportiveness, and psychological autonomy.

(4) The academic performance of children from the families with low SES but high parental monitoring, supportiveness and psychological autonomy would not differ from that of children from the families with high SES but low parental monitoring, supportiveness, and psychological autonomy.

(5) Children from intact families and high SES would report having more parental monitoring, support and psychological autonomy.

Based on an integrated research paradigm, the direct and indirect effects of family structure and SES on children's academic performance were examined. The mediating effects of the three dimensions of authoritative parenting style on children's academic achievement were also investigated.

III

Method

The need for an integrated research strategy that incorporates both family status and process variables, presented in the preceding chapters, serves as the general rationale for the study reported in this book. Specifically, the study examined the effects of family structure, socioeconomic status, and three dimensions (parental monitoring, parental supportiveness, and psychological autonomy) of authoritative parenting style on children's academic achievement.

THE SAMPLE

The subjects of this study were 181 8th graders from two middle schools in the Minneapolis Public School District. They were a sub-sample from a 5-year (1990-95) dropout prevention project jointly conducted by the University of Minnesota and the Minneapolis Public School District.* All subjects were 8th

---

* The full title of the project was Dropout Prevention and Intervention programs for Junior High School Students in Special Education. The principal investigators were Sandra Christenson, Ph.D., Martha Thurlow, Ph.D., and Robert H. Bruininks, Ph.D. This project was funded by the Office of Special Education Programs, U.S. Department of Education (H023K0017).

graders in regular education selected by a stratified random sampling procedure. To ensure that the sample included subjects from a wide range of socioeconomic backgrounds, half of the students were selected randomly from a population of students who were eligible for a free/reduced price lunch program and half were selected randomly from those who were not. A list of 311 students was generated by this procedure. Ten students and their parents refused to participate and sixteen students moved out of the school district during the investigation. Among the remaining 285 students, 213 had complete information on all the measures. Thirty-two of these 213 students were from step-families or single-father families. They were excluded in the analysis since these subtypes of two-parent and single-parent families differ in their association with children's adjustment (Zimiles & Lee, 1991). As a result, the subjects of this study were 181 8th graders. Their average age was 14 years old. Additional demographic data of these subjects is presented in Table 1.

Table 1
Demographic Data of the Subjects

	Family Structure		
	Intact Families	Single-Mother Families	Total
Number	98	83	181
Percentage	54.1%	45.9%	100%

Table 1 continued.

| | Sex | | |
	Male	Female	Total
Intact Families			
Number	44	54	98
Percentage	44.9%	55.1%	100%
Single-Mother Families			
Number	37	46	83
Percentage	44.6%	55.4%	100%
Total			
Number	81	100	181
Percentage	44.8%	55.2%	100%

| | Ethnicity | | |
	Intact Families	Single-Mother Families	Total
Native Americans			
Number	4	3	7
Percentage	4.1%	3.6%	3.9%
African Americans			
Number	19	45%	64
Percentage	10.4%	54.2%	35.4%
Asian Americans			
Number	7	0	7
Percentage	7.1%	0%	3.9%
Hispanic Americans			
Number	5	0	5
Percentage	5.1%	0%	2.8%
Caucasian Americans			
Number	63	35	98
Percentage	64.3%	42.2%	54.0%
Total			
Number	98	83	181
Percentage	100%	100%	100%

MEASURES

The social address paradigm, family process paradigm and an integrated paradigm were employed to examine the influences of the family on children's academic achievement. The social address variables examined in this study were Family Structure (FS) and Socioeconomic Status (SES). The family process variables were the three dimensions of authoritative parenting: Parental Monitoring (MON), Supportiveness (SUP), and Psychological Autonomy (AUT). The outcome variable was Children's Academic Achievement.

Social Address Variables

Family Structure (FS) specifies one of two family configurations: single-mother or intact families. A single-mother family was defined as a family in which the biological mother was the only parent living with the adolescent in the household. An intact family was defined as a family in which both biological parents were living with the adolescent in the household. Step families and single-father families were excluded from the present study.

Socioeconomic Status (SES) was measured by 1) occupational level of parents (OCC), 2) educational level of the parents (EDU), and 3) income level of parents (INC). The occupational level of parents was defined by the Duncun Socioeconomic Index (Stevens & Cho, 1985). This index was developed in the mid- 1980s to estimate prestige ratings for census occupations not included in the previous Duncun scale and was based on data from the 1980 census. The scores in the

Table 2

Socioeconomic Background of the Subjects

	M	SD
Intact Families		
Occupational Level	41.99	20.97
Educational Level	5.95	1.40
Income Level	$42,803	$23,964
Single-Mother Families		
Occupational Level	28.42	16.83
Educational Level	5.46	1.08
Income Level	$20,165	$12,793
Total		
Occupational Level	35.76	20.30
Educational Level	5.72	1.28
Income Level	$32,422	$22,626

Note: M = Mean, SD = Standard Deviation.

present scale range from 13.98 (winding and twisting machine operators) to 90.45 (law school professor). The Duncan Socioeconomic Index was recommended by Mueller and Parcel (1981) as one of the best measures of SES of individuals or household heads. The scores of the parents' educational level (EDU) ranged from 1 to 8 (1 = less than 7th grade, 2 = 7th to 8th grade, 3 = 9th grade, 4 = 10th to 11th grade, 5 = high school graduate, 6 = some college, 7 = college graduate, and 8 = graduate school). Income level (INC) was the total family income before taxes in 1992. Occupational level, educational level, and income level were selected because they are the traditional measures of SES. Moreover, as mentioned in Chapter II, measures of SES that combine two or more indicators are more highly correlated with academic achievement than any single indicator (White, 1982). A composite SES score was computed for each family by adding the z scores of OCC, EDU, and INC. Parental self-report was the source of information for the OCC, EDU, and INC variables. For a family with two working parents, the highest Duncan Socioeconomic Index of either parent would be taken as the family OCC. The same rule was applied to the EDU variable; the highest educational level achieved by either parent would be considered as the educational level of both parents for that family. The socioeconomic background of the children in this study is presented in Table 2.

Family Process Variables

Parental monitoring (MON), parental supportiveness (SUP), and psychological autonomy (AUT) are three constructs of authoritative parenting style. Parental monitoring (MON) is a construct that specifies the extent to which parents provide and enforce clear and consistent guidelines and rules for a child's behavior. Parental supportiveness (SUP) is a construct specifying the extent to which parents are loving, responsive, and involved with their children. Psychological autonomy (AUT) is a construct specifying the extent to which parents employ noncoercive democratic discipline and encourage their children to express individuality within the family. MON, SUP, and AUT are similar to the dimensions of parental strictness/supervision, parental warmth/involvement, and psychological autonomy in the terminology used by Steinberg, et al. (1991). Data on the parental monitoring (MON), parental supportiveness (SUP),and psychological autonomy (AUT) constructs were collected by a questionnaire survey. The Parent-Child Interaction Questionnaire (PCIQ) (see Appendix A) was developed from the items used by Dornbusch, et al. (1987). and Steinberg et al. (1991). Appendix B provides a list of the PCIQ items, indicating which items were adapted from Dornbusch et al. (1987) and which items were adapted from Steinberg et al. (1991). Three factors emerged when Steinberg, et al. (1991) subjected their items to exploratory factor analyses using an oblique rotation: firm control, acceptance/ involvement, and psychological autonomy. In their study, the firm control scale measured parental monitoring and limit setting. It consisted of nine items and the coefficient alpha was .76. The acceptance/involvement scale measured the extent to which the adolescent perceived his or her parents as loving, responsive and involved. It consisted of 15 items and the coefficient alpha was .72. The psychological autonomy scale assessed the extent to which parents employed noncoercive, democratic discipline and encouraged the adolescent to express individuality within the family. It consisted of 12 items and the coefficient alpha was .72.

Table 3
Coefficient Alpha for Each Scale on the Parent-Child Interaction Questionnaire

Scales	Number of Items	Coefficient Alphas
MON	8	.68
SUP	12	.82
AUT	10	.63

The scales of the Parent-Child Interaction Questionnaires (PCIQ) were based on the work of Steinberg et al. (1991). The items in the PCIQ were divided into three scales: MON, SUP, and AUT. They corresponded to the firm control, acceptance/involvement, and psychological autonomy scales employed by Steinberg et al. (1991). Scores were obtained for these scales according to the responses given by the respondents. Based on the data in this study, the coefficient alpha for each of the scales on the PCIQ is presented in Table 3.

Outcome Variable

Academic achievement of the children was measured by their grade point averages (GPAs) of the current school year. A twelve-point system was used to transform the letter grade to a grade point (A+ = 12, A = 11, A- = 10, B+ = 9, B = 8, B- = 7, C+ = 6, C = 5, C- = 4, D+ = 3, D = 2, D- = 1, F = 0). The GPAs of the students were retrieved from their school records in June 1993.

PROCEDURE

At the beginning of the 1992-93 school year, letters from the *Dropout Prevention Project* were sent to all parents of the students in the two participating middle schools, asking permission for their children to participate in the research project. A negative consent form was used. Parents who did not want their children to participate would send in the negative consent form. The subjects of the present study were selected from among the students whose parents did not send in the negative consent form.

The children filled out the Parent-Child Interaction Questionnaire (see appendix A) at school in April 1993.

Classroom teachers read each item of the questionnaire out loud, to avoid the possibility that reading problems would interfere with the children's understanding of the questions. Information on socioeconomic background was obtained through telephone interviews with parents while other information for a related study was collected. A demographic data sheet (see appendix C) was completed during each interview. The interviews were conducted by two graduate students in February, March, and April 1993. The parents who had no telephone were visited at home. About 10% of the interviews were conducted at home instead of by phone.

STATISTICAL ANALYSES

The data of the study were analyzed by the SPSS package. The statistical procedures included *t*-tests, analysis of variance, bi-variate correlation, and path analysis. Multiple regression is commonly used to examine relationships between a dependent variable and a set of independent variables. However, this study employed path analysis instead of multiple regression to examine the direct and indirect effects of socioeconomic status, family structure, and authoritative parenting on children's academic achievement. Multiple regression allows for correlations among independent variables but does not permit the researcher to specify causal relationships among these variables (see Figure 4). Mediating effects, if any, of some predictor variables cannot be examined since any given variable is either an independent or a dependent variable, and only one dependent variable can be specified.

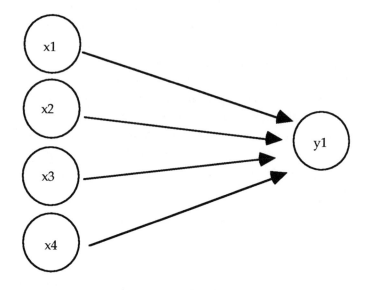

Figure 4. Multiple regression where x1 to x4 are independent variables and y1 is the dependent variable.

Compared to multiple regression, path analysis allows for the specification of causal relationships among the predictor variables. Since a given variable can be both a cause of some variables and an effect of others, both direct and indirect effects of predictor variables can be examined (see Figure 5).

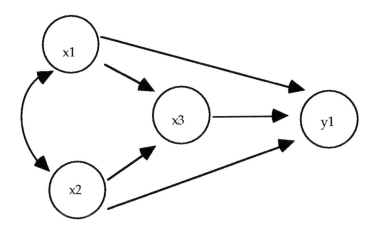

Figure 5. Path analysis where x1, x2 are independent variables, y1 is a dependent variable, and x3 is both an independent and dependent variable.

Since path analysis allows for a richer complex of mediational models than does multiple regression, this study employed path analysis to address the questions formulated in the integrated research paradigm. In this way, both direct and indirect effects of family structure and SES on children's academic performance could be examined. The mediating effects of the three dimensions of authoritative parenting on children's academic achievement could also be investigated. The procedure described by Alwin and Hauser (1975) was adopted to decompose separate effects in the path analysis.

IV

Results

The relationships among family structure, socioeconomic status, authoritative parenting, and children's academic achievement was investigated in a sample of 181 8th graders in two inner-city schools in the midwestern United States. How the family influences children's academic achievement was first examined with a social address paradigm, then with a family process paradigm. The interactive effects of social address and family process on children's academic achievement were subsequently examined with an integrated paradigm using path analysis.

ANALYSES IN SOCIAL ADDRESS PARADIGM

Family Structure and Academic Achievement

The mean Grade Point Averages (GPAs) of the children from intact and single-mother families are presented in Table 4. Children from intact families had significantly higher GPAs than did children from single-mother families, $t = 5.70$, $df = 179$, $p < 0.01$.

Table 4
Mean GPAs of the Children from Intact and Single-Mother Families

Family Structure	M	SD	N
Intact	8.736	2.186	98
Single-Mother	6.668	2.693	83

Socioeconomic Status and Academic Achievement

The children in this study were subdivided into three socioeconomic groups according to their SES scores. The children whose SES scores were above or equal to the 66.67th percentile were assigned to the high SES group. The children whose SES scores were below the 66.67th percentile but above or equal to the 33.33th percentile were assigned to the medium SES group. The rest of the children had SES scores lower than the 33.33th percentile and were assigned to the low SES group.

Table 5 presents the GPAs of the children from different SES groups. It was found that children from different SES groups had significantly different GPAs, $F(2, 178) = 29.88, p < 0.01$. The results of post-hoc test of Scheffe at 0.05 significant level indicated that the children from the high SES group had higher GPAs than did children from medium and low SES groups. The children from the medium SES group also had higher GPAs than did children from the low SES group.

Table 5
Mean GPAs Obtained by Children from Different SES Groups

SES	M	SD	N
Low	5.965	2.363	60
Medium	8.328	2.136	61
High	9.060	2.375	60

Family Structure, Socioeconomic Status, and Academic Achievement

The mean GPAs of the children in the two family structure groups and three SES are presented in Table 6. A two-way analysis of variance was performed on the data (see Table 7). It was found that both family structure and SES had significant effects on GPA. However, there was no interaction effect between family structure and SES (see Table 7 and Figure 3). The effects of family structure on GPA did not vary across different SES groups. Children from intact families with high SES tended to have higher GPAs than did children from single-mother families with low SES. Nevertheless, it is noteworthy that the mean GPA of the children from intact families with low SES ($M = 7.09$, $SD = 1.95$) was not significantly different from that of their counterparts from single-mother families with high SES ($M = 8.42$, $SD = 2.88$), $t = 1.48$, $df = 27$, $p = 0.182$.

Table 6
Mean GPAs of Children by Family Structure and SES

SES	Intact Families	Single-Mother Families
Low		
M	7.09	5.52
SD	1.95	2.38
N	17	43
Medium		
M	8.88	7.68
SD	1.85	2.30
N	33	28
High		
M	9.22	8.42
SD	2.24	2.88
N	48	12

Table 7
Results of Two-way ANOVA on GPA by Family Structure and SES

Source	df	F. Ratio
Main Effect	3	24.53**
Family Structure	1	10.93**
SES	2	17.62**
Interaction	2	0.31
Error	175	(5.017)

Note: Value in parenthesis represents mean square error.
**$p < .01$

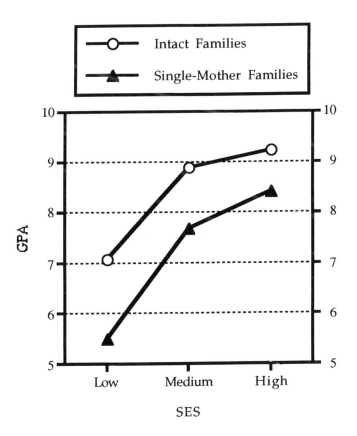

Figure 6. GPAs of children from intact and single-mother families across different SES groups.

ANALYSES IN FAMILY PROCESS PARADIGM

In the social address paradigm, the focus is on the relationship between social address variables and children's academic achievement. In this section, the family process paradigm is employed. The focus of the analyses is the relationship between family process variables and children's academic achievement.

Authoritative Parenting and Academic Achievement

The three dimensions of authoritative parenting are parental monitoring, parental supportiveness, and psychological autonomy. In this study, they were measured by the Parent-Child Interaction Questionnaire (PCIQ). The scores on the scales of Parental Monitoring (MON), Parental Supportiveness (SUP), and Psychological Autonomy (AUT) in the PCIQ respectively reflected the degree to which a child reported he/she had parental monitoring, parental supportiveness, and psychological autonomy. The higher these scores, the more parental monitoring, parental supportiveness, and psychological autonomy the child reported.

The children in this study were subdivided into three groups according to their scores on the Parental Monitoring scale. The children whose scores were above or equivalent to the 66.67th percentile were assigned to the high Parental Monitoring group. The children whose score were below the 66.67th percentile but above or equivalent to the 33.33th percentile were assigned to the medium Parental Monitoring group. The rest of the children, whose scores were below the 33.33th percentile, were assigned to the low Parental Monitoring group. A one-way analysis of variance was performed on the GPAs of these three groups of children (see Table 8). The children who reported having different levels of parental monitoring differed significantly in their GPAs, $F(2, 178) = 11.102$, $p < .01$. Post-hoc Scheffe tests at 0.05 level revealed that the children in the high and medium Parental Monitoring groups had significantly higher GPAs than those in the low Parental Monitoring group.

The children in this study were also subdivided into three groups according to their scores on the Parental Supportiveness scale (SUP) in the PCIQ. Correspondingly, it was found that the children who reported different levels of parental supportiveness differed significantly in their GPAs, $F(2, 178) = 17.726$, $p < .01$ (see Table 8). Post-hoc Scheffe tests at 0.05 level revealed that the children in the high Parental Supportiveness group had significantly higher GPAs than those in the medium and low Parental Supportiveness groups.

The same comparison was performed on children in the high, medium and low Psychological Autonomy groups. Similar results were found. The children who reported different levels of psychological autonomy differed significantly in GPAs, $F(2,178) = 11.415$, $p < 0.01$ (see Table 8). Post-hoc Scheffe tests at 0.05 level revealed that the children in the high Psychological Autonomy group had significantly higher GPAs than their counterparts in the medium and low Psychological Autonomy groups.

Table 8
*Results of One-Way ANOVAs on GPA for the Low, Medium,
and High Subgroups of Parental Monitoring, Parental
Supportiveness, and Psychological Autonomy*

Dimensions of Authoritative Parenting	Low	Medium	High	F Value
Parental Monitoring				
M	6.53	7.87	8.76	11.102**
SD	2.51	2.57	2.40	
N	51	70	60	
Parental Supportiveness				
M	6.68	7.30	9.18	17.726**
SD	2.47	2.71	2.07	
N	55	65	65	
Psychological Autonomy				
M	6.66	7.76	8.87	11.415**
SD	2.51	2.46	2.46	
N	56	65	60	

**$p < .01$

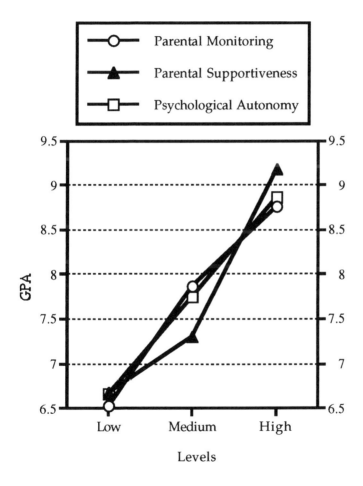

Figure 7. GPAs of children who reported different levels of parental monitoring, parental supportiveness, and psychological autonomy.

Authoritative Parenting, Family Structure and Academic Achievement

When the academic achievement of the children was examined in social address paradigm, it was found to be significantly associated with family structure. Children from intact families had higher GPAs than their counterparts in single-mother families. However, this association was mediated by family process variables. As shown in Table 9, the GPAs of the children from single-mother families with high parental monitoring (M = 7.93, SD = 2.64) were not significantly different from those of children from intact families with low parental monitoring (M = 7.69, SD = 2.09), $t = -.35$, df = 46, $p = 0.729$.

Table 9
GPAs of Children from Intact and Single-Mother Families with different levels of Parental Monitoring

| | | Parental Monitoring | |
Family Structure	Low	Medium	High
Intact			
M	7.69	8.8	9.36
SD	2.09	2.18	9.36
N	23	40	35
Single-Mother			
M	5.57	6.64	7.93
SD	2.46	2.56	2.64
N	28	30	25

The same pattern was observed in the relationship between parental supportiveness and family structure. As shown in Table 10, the GPAs of the children from single-mother families with high parental supportiveness (M = 8.04, SD = 2.45) were not significantly different from those of the children from intact families with low parental supportiveness (M = 7.33, SD = 2.11), $t = -.96$, df = 38, $p = 0.343$.

Table 10
GPAs of Children from Intact and Single-Mother Families with Different Levels of Parental Supportiveness

| | Parental Supportiveness | | |
Family Structure	Low	Medium	High
Intact			
M	7.33	8.20	9.80
SD	2.11	2.32	1.52
N	17	39	42
Single-Mother			
M	6.39	5.72	8.04
SD	2.58	2.67	2.45
N	38	22	23

Similarly, the GPAs of the children from single-mother families with high psychological autonomy (M = 7.26, SD = 2.90) were not different from those of the children from intact families with low psychological autonomy (M = 7.43, SD = 2.25), $t = .22$, df = 42, $p = 0.829$ (see Table 11).

Table 11

GPAs of Children from Intact and Single-Mother Families with Different Levels of Psychological Autonomy

Family Structure	Psychological Autonomy		
	Low	Medium	High
Intact			
M	7.43	8.48	9.74
SD	2.25	2.18	1.65
N	23	36	39
Single-Mother			
M	6.12	6.86	7.26
SD	2.59	2.63	2.90
N	33	29	21

Authoritative Parenting, Socioeconomic Status, and Academic Achievement

In the social address paradigm, socioeconomic status (SES) was significantly associated with children's academic achievement. The GPAs of the children from families with high SES were significantly higher than those of the children from families with low SES. However, this association was also mediated by family process variables.

In this study, the GPAs of the children from families with low SES but high parental monitoring (M = 6.11, SD = 2.24), as shown in Table 12, were not significantly different from those of the children from families with high SES but low parental monitoring (M = 6.50, SD = 2.75), $t = -.38$, df = 21, $p = .711$.

Table 12

GPAs of Children from Low, Medium, and High SES Groups with Different Levels of Parental Monitoring

SES	Parental Monitoring		
	Low	Medium	High
Low			
M	5.83	6.01	6.11
SD	2.61	2.27	2.24
N	23	23	14
Medium			
M	7.38	8.67	8.83
SD	2.11	2.18	1.94
N	19	19	23
High			
M	6.50	8.85	10.31
SD	2.75	2.25	1.33
N	9	28	23

Similarly, parental supportiveness also mediated the association between SES and children's academic achievement. In spite of the fact that children from high SES group had higher GPAs, children from families with low SES but high parental supportiveness (M = 6.71, SD = 1.69) did not have significantly lower GPAs than their counterparts from families with high SES but low parental supportiveness (M = 6.32, SD = 2.37), $t = -.43$, df = 18, $p = .675$ (see Table 13).

Table 13

GPAs of Children from Low, Medium, and High SES Groups with Different Levels of Parental Supportiveness

SES	Parental Supportiveness		
	Low	Medium	High
Low			
M	5.93	5.64	6.71
SD	2.45	2.54	1.69
N	27	22	11
Medium			
M	7.92	7.71	9.18
SD	2.13	2.29	1.80
N	19	19	23
High			
M	6.32	8.75	10.05
SD	2.37	2.35	1.66
N	9	20	31

The same pattern appeared again in the effect of psychological autonomy on the association between SES and GPA. The GPAs of the children from families with low SES but high psychological autonomy (M = 5.67, SD = 2.04) did not differ significantly from those of the children from families with high SES but low psychological autonomy (M = 6.52, SD = 2.30), t = -.87, df = 18, p = .393 (see Table 14).

Table 14

GPAs of Children from Low, Medium, and High SES Groups with Different Levels of Psychological Autonomy

SES	Psychological Autonomy		
	Low	Medium	High
Low			
M	5.88	6.20	5.67
SD	2.56	2.31	2.04
N	28	22	10
Medium			
M	7.94	8.44	8.54
SD	2.15	1.91	2.39
N	18	22	21
High			
M	6.52	8.67	10.22
SD	2.30	2.57	1.29
N	10	21	29

ANALYSES IN INTEGRATED PARADIGM

As shown in the previous section, family process variables could mediate the association between social address variables and children's academic achievement. However, there is still a need to examine how family process variables interact with social address variables in influencing school performance. In the first half of this section, the relationship between family structure, SES, and authoritative parenting is examined. In the second half, path analysis is used to investigate the interactive effects of these variables on children's academic achievement.

Family Structure and Authoritative Parenting

While family structure and authoritative parenting were associated with children's academic achievement, family structure and authoritative parenting were also related.

Children from intact families reported having significantly more parental monitoring, parental supportiveness, and psychological autonomy (see Table 15 and Figure 8).

Table 15
Raw Scores on the MON, SUP, and AUT Scales for Children from Intact and Single-Mother Families

Dimensions of Authoritative Parenting	Intact Families	Single-Mother Families	*t* Value
Parental Monitoring			
M	30.87	28.84	2.48*
SD	5.25	5.73	
N	98	83	
Parental Supportiveness	45.81	43.12	3.04**
M	5.77	6.08	
SD	98	83	
N			
Psychological Autonomy			
M	33.74	31.31	2.94**
SD	5.31	5.83	
N	98	83	

* *p* < .05.   ** *p* < .01.

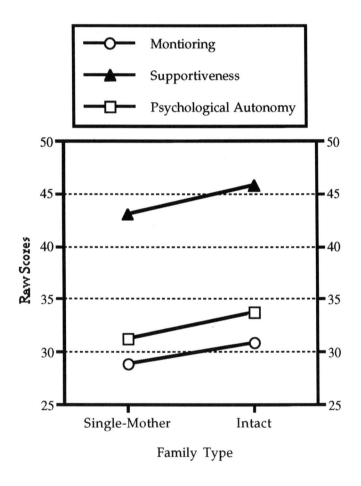

Figure 8. Raw scores on the MON, SUP, and AUT scales for children from intact and single-mother families.

Socioeconomic Status and Authoritative Parenting

A distinct pattern was also found in the relationship between SES and authoritative parenting. While both SES and authoritative parenting were associated with children's academic achievement, these factors themselves were highly correlated. The children from families with different SES levels reported significantly different degrees of parental monitoring, $F(2, 178) = 4.497, p = .012$. They also reported significantly different degrees of parental supportiveness, $F (2, 178) = 9.845, p < 0.01$. The same pattern also applied to psychological autonomy, $F (2, 178) = 12.506, p < 0.01$. In general, the children from families with high SES reported more parental monitoring, parental supportiveness, and psychological autonomy than the children from families with low SES (see Table 16 and Figure 9).

Table 16

Raw Scores on the MON, SUP, and AUT Scales for Children from Low, Medium, and High SES Groups

Dimensions of Authoritative Parenting	Socioeconomic Status			F Value
	Low	Medium	High	
Parental Monitoring				
M	28.46	29.93	31.44	4.497*
SD	5.64	6.02	4.57	
N	60	61	60	
Parental Supportiveness				
M	42.21	44.63	46.88	9.845**
SD	5.33	6.65	5.20	
N	60	61	60	
Psychological Autonomy				
M	30.08	32.84	43.94	12.506**
SD	5.03	5.747	5.74	
N	60	61	60	

* $p < .05$. ** $p < .01$.

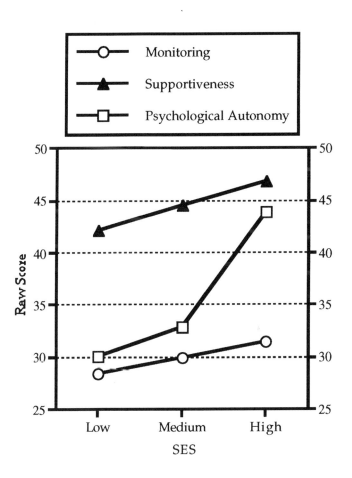

Figure 9. Raw scores on the MON, SUP, and AUT scales for children from low, medium, and high SES groups.

Path Analysis

In this section, path analysis is employed to examine the direct and indirect effects of family structure and SES on children's academic achievement. The mediating effects of the three dimensions of authoritative parenting style on children's academic achievement are also investigated. The procedure described by Alwin and Hauser (1975) is adopted to decompose effects in the path analysis.

Table 17 is the correlation matrix of the variables in the path analysis.

Table 17
Correlation Matrix of the Variables in the Path Analysis

	SES	FS	MON	SUP	AUT	GPA
SES	1.000					
FS	.384**	1.000				
MON	.256**	.183*	1.000			
SUP	.306**	.222*	.390**	1.000		
AUT	.366**	.214*	.263**	.612**	1.000	
GPA	.471**	.392**	.350**	.384**	.382**	1.000

*$p < .05$ ** $p < .01$

Legends:
SES   Socioeconomic Status
FS   Family Structure
MON   Parental Monitoring
SUP   Parental Supportiveness
AUT   Psychological Autonomy
GPA   Grade Point Average

Table 18
Effects of Socioeconomic Status and Family Structure on Children's Academic Achievement

	Socioeconomic Status	Family Structure
Total Association	.471	.392
Total Effects	.375 (100%)	.248 (100%)
Indirect Effect via MON, SUP & AUT	.108 (28.8%)	.041 (16.5%)
Direct Effects	.267 (71.2%)	.207 (83.4%)

Note: Numbers in parentheses are the percentages of the total effects constituted by the indirect or direct effect.

As shown in Table 18, the total association between SES and GPA was .471. The total effects of SES on GPA were .375. While 71.2% of the total effects of SES on GPA were direct effects, 28.8% of them were indirect effect mediated by parental monitoring, parental supportiveness, and psychological autonomy. The direct and indirect effects of SES on GPA were .267 and .108 respectively.

The total association between family structure and GPA was .392. The total effects of family structure on GPA were .248. While 83.5% of the total effects of family structure on GPA were direct, 16.5% of them were indirectly mediated by the three dimensions of authoritative parenting. The direct and indirect effects of family structure on GPA were .207 and .041 respectively.

Table 19

Effects of Parental Monitoring, Parental Supportiveness, and Psychological Autonomy on GPA

	Parental Monitoring	Parental Supportiveness	Psychological Autonomy
Total Association	.350 (100%)	.384 (100%)	.382 (100%)
Non-Causal Effects	.184 (52.6%)	.270 (70.3%)	.255 (66.8%)
Causal Effects	.166 (47.4%)	.114 (29.7%)	.127 (33.2%)

Note: Numbers in the parentheses are the percentages of the total association constituted by the non-causal or causal effects.

As shown in Table 19, the total association between parental monitoring and GPA was .350. While 52.6% were non-causal effects due to the effects of family structure and SES, 47.4% were shown to be causal when the effects of family structure and SES were partialled out. The non-causal and causal effects of parental monitoring on GPA were .184 and .166 respectively. The total association between parental supportiveness and GPA was .384. While 70.3% were non-causal effects due to the effects of family structure and SES, 29.7% were seen to be causal when the effects of family structure and SES were partialled out. The non-causal and causal effects of parental supportiveness on GPA were .270 and .114 respectively. The total association between psychological autonomy and GPA was .382. While 66.8% were non-causal effects due to the influences of family structure and SES, 33.2% were shown to be causal effects when the effects of family structure and SES were partialled out. The non-causal and causal effects of psychological autonomy on GPA were .255 and .127 respectively.

Table 20
Effects of Family Structure on Parental Monitoring, Parental Supportiveness, and Psychological Autonomy

	Parental Monitoring	Parental Supportiveness	Psychological Autonomy
Total Association	.183 (100%)	.260 (100%)	.214 (100%)
Total Effects	.099 (54.1%)	.122 (46.9%)	.087 (40.7%)
Non Causal Effects	.084 (45.9%)	.138 (53.1%)	.127 (59.3%)

Note: Numbers in the parentheses are the percentages of the total association constituted by the total or non-causal effects.

As shown in Table 20, the total association between family structure and parental monitoring was .183. The total effects of family structure on parental monitoring were .099 when the effects of SES were partialled out. The total effects comprised only 54.1% of the total association. About 45% of the total association between family structure and parental monitoring was due to the influences of SES. The total association between family structure and parental supportiveness was .260. The total effects of family structure on parental supportiveness were .122 when the effects of SES were partialled out. The total effects comprised only 46.9% of the total association. About 55% of the total association between family structure and parental supportiveness were due to the influences of SES. The total association between family structure and psychological autonomy was .214. The total effects of family structure on psychological autonomy were .087 when the effects of SES were partialled out. Similarly, the total effects comprised only 40% of the total association. About 59% of the total association between family structure and psychological autonomy was due to the effects of SES.

Table 21
Effects of SES on Parental Monitoring, Parental Supportiveness, and Psychological Autonomy

	Parental Monitoring	Parental Supportiveness	Psychological Autonomy
Total Association	.256 (100%)	.306 (100%)	.366 (100%)
Total Effects	.217 (85.8%)	.260 (85.0%)	.332 (90.7%)
Non-Causal Effects	.039 (14.2%)	.046 (15.0%)	.034 (9.3%)

Note: Numbers in parentheses are the percentages of the total association constituted by the total or non causal effects.

As shown in Table 21, the total association between SES and parental monitoring was .256. The total effects of SES on parental monitoring were .217 when the effects of family structure were partialled out. These were 85.8% of the total association between SES and parental monitoring. In other words, 14.2% of the total association between SES and parental monitoring was due to the effects of family structure. The total association between SES and parental supportiveness was .306. The total effects of SES on parental supportiveness was .260 when the effects of family structure were partialled out. They comprised 85% of the total association. Only 15% of the total association between SES and parental supportiveness was due to the effects of family structure. The total association between SES and psychological autonomy was .366. The total effects of SES on psychological autonomy were .332 when the effects of family structure were partialled out. They comprised 90.7% of the total association. Only less than 10% of the total association between SES and psychological autonomy was due to the effects of family structure.

Based on the decomposed effects presented in Tables 18 to 21, a path diagram with path coefficients was constructed to show the relationships between family structure, socioeconomic status, parental monitoring, parental supportiveness, psychological autonomy and children's academic achievement (see Figure 10). In the present study, the combined social address and family process variables explained 35.7% of the variance of the children's academic achievement.

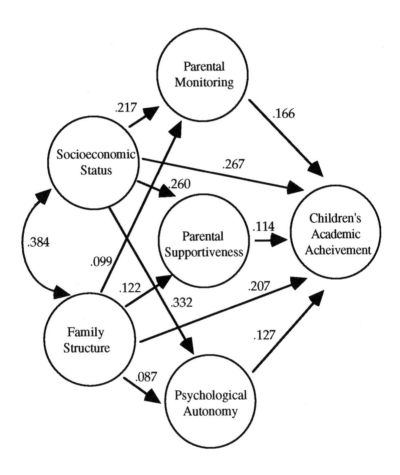

Figure 10. Path diagram of the relationships between family structure, socioeconomic status, parental monitoring, parental supportiveness, psychological autonomy, and children's academic achievement.

V

Discussion

As the reader will recall, five hypotheses about the influences of the family on children's academic achievement were formulated in Chapter II. These hypotheses were based on three research paradigms that employ social address, family process, or an integrated perspective. In this chapter, the results relevant to each of these hypotheses are discussed and applied to an evaluation of the efficacy of each of the three research paradigms.

SOCIAL ADDRESS PARADIGM

The first research paradigm under scrutiny is the social address paradigm in which the academic achievement of children from different social addresses are compared. The focus of the inquiry is on the effects of family structure and SES on children's academic achievement.

Family Structure, Socioeconomic Status, and Academic Achievement

According to the social address paradigm, it was hypothesized that children from intact families with high SES would have higher academic performance than children from single-mother families with low socioeconomic background. As shown in chapter IV, this hypothesis was supported by the data in this study. Children from intact families had significantly higher GPAs than did children from single-mother families. Children from families with high SES also had significantly higher GPAs than did children from families with medium or low SES. The results showed evidence of the influences of family structure and SES on children's academic achievement. They also showed evidence of the efficacy of the social address paradigm. Children from different social addresses or ecological niches attained different levels of academic achievement.

However, it is noteworthy that the GPAs of the children from intact families with low SES was not significantly different from those of children from single-mother families with high SES. This finding indicates that neither family structure nor SES has determining effects on children's academic achievement. Children from single-mother families with high socioeconomic background did not show lower achievement than their counterparts in intact families. Similarly, children from families with low SES did not achieve less than their counterparts from families with high SES, if they were from intact instead of single-mother families. Without looking into the effects of family structure and SES simultaneously, researchers cannot make unqualified conclusions about either of them. The complexity of the influences of the family on children's academic achievement are apparent when two or more family status variables are taken into consideration.

In the social address paradigm, no matter how many family status variables are included in various investigations, researchers are still unable to explain why children from different social addresses are routinely found to have different levels of academic achievement. As Bronfenbrenner and Crouter (1983) have pointed out, when researchers rely solely on the social address paradigm, they look only at the environmental label and "pay no attention to what the environment is like, what people are living there, what they are doing, or how the activities taking place could affect the child." (pp. 361-2). In another words, social address researchers give no explicit consideration to intervening processes through which the social address might affect the development of children. When intervening processes are ignored, observed differences between children from different social address are left explained.

FAMILY PROCESS PARADIGM

Compared to the social address paradigm, the family process paradigm has the obvious advantage of emphasizing the role of more direct processes in the immediate environment that influence children. In the family process paradigm, the focus of investigation is shifted from family status variables to family process variables; the relationships between family processes and children's developmental outcomes become the main concern.

Authoritative Parenting and Academic Achievement

According to the family process paradigm, it was hypothesized that children who reported having more parental monitoring, parental supportiveness, and psychological autonomy would have higher academic performance than those who reported having less parental monitoring, parental supportiveness, and psychological autonomy. The hypothesis was supported by the results of the present study. Children who reported high or medium parental monitoring attained significantly higher GPAs than those who reported low parental monitoring. Children who reported high parental supportiveness attained significantly higher GPAs than those who reported medium or low parental supportiveness. Similarly, children who reported high psychological autonomy attained significantly higher GPAs than those who reported medium or low psychological autonomy.

The results provide evidence that authoritative parenting contributes to differences in academic achievement among children. This finding gains more support when the effects of authoritative parenting are examined in combination with those of family structure and SES.

Authoritative Parenting, Family Structure and Academic Achievement

When children's academic achievement was examined in the social address paradigm, it was found to be significantly associated with family structure. However, this association was mediated by family process variables. According to the family process paradigm, it was hypothesized that the academic performance of children from single-mother families with high parental monitoring, supportiveness, and psychological autonomy would not differ from that of children from intact families with low parental monitoring, supportiveness, and psychological autonomy. This hypothesis was supported by the data: It was found that GPAs of children from single-mother families with high parental monitoring, high parental supportiveness, and high psychological autonomy were not different from GPAs of children from intact families with low parental monitoring, low parental supportiveness, and low psychological autonomy.

Authoritative Parenting, SES and Academic Achievement

In spite of the fact that SES was found to be significantly associated with children's academic achievement in the social address paradigm, this association was mediated by authoritative parenting. According to the family process paradigm, it was hypothesized that the academic performance of children from families with low SES but high parental monitoring, high supportiveness, and high psychological autonomy would not differ from that of children from the families with high SES but low parental monitoring, low supportiveness, and low psychological autonomy. Consistent with what was found about the relationships between family structure, authoritative parenting, and academic achievement, this hypothesis was supported by the data. In this study, the GPAs of children from families with low SES but high parental monitoring, high parental supportiveness, and high psychological autonomy were not significantly different from those of the children from families with high SES but low parental monitoring, low parental supportiveness, and low psychological autonomy.

The data in this study provide evidence that developmental outcomes of children are not solely determined by family status variables, such as family structure, and SES. Children from single-mother families with low SES do not necessarily achieve less than children from intact families with high SES. The developmental outcomes of children depend on the family processes taking place in the social address of concern. If authoritative parenting is practised, children from single-mother families or low socioeconomic backgrounds will not necessarily achieve less than their counterparts from intact families or those with high socioeconomic backgrounds. However, the same evidence also indicates that researchers cannot conclude that developmental outcomes are solely determined by family processes. The results of this study show that even when authoritative parenting is practised, children will not necessarily have high academic performance if they are from single-mother families or low socioeconomic backgrounds.

The obvious conclusion is that researchers need to investigate the effects of both family status and processes variables. Investigating either set of variables separately can only provide an incomplete picture. In the social address paradigm, family status variables are consistently found to be associated with the developmental outcomes of children. The data support the conclusion that family structure and SES have significant effects on children's academic achievement. This finding was consistent with the findings of previous studies which also employed the social address paradigm (Amber & Saucier, 1984; Featherstone et al., 1992; Mueller & Cooper, 1986; Zimiles & Lee, 1991). On the other hand, within the family process paradigm, family process variables are also consistently found to be associated with the developmental outcomes of children. When the family process paradigm was used, the data in the present study supported the conclusion that authoritative parenting has a significant impact on children's academic achievement. This finding is consistent with the findings of previous studies which have employed the family process paradigm (Dornbusch, et al., 1987; Lamborn et, al., 1991; Steinberg et al., 1989; Grolnick & Ryan, 1989). Focusing on one set of variables while ignoring the other set of variables is unlikely to help researchers understand the complexity of the influences of families on children. Each research paradigm directs the attention of researchers to only part of the reality. When either research paradigm is employed separately, researchers will continue to find that social address variables and family process variables each have impact on children's developmental outcomes. However, little is known how these two set of variables are related and how they interactively affect children. This limitation highlights the need to integrate the two research paradigms in investigations of family influences on children's developmental outcomes.

INTEGRATED PARADIGM

Family process and family status variables are not two sets of unrelated and independent variables. As Halsey (1975) points out, parental attitude should be conceived as an integral part of the work and community situation of children. Kohn (1979) also argues that child-rearing practices of parents must be seen in terms of the realities they face. Family processes are not independent of family status. The findings of the present study strongly support the claims of Halsey and Kohn.

Family Structure, SES and Authoritative Parenting

According to the integrated paradigm, it was hypothesized that children from intact families and high socioeconomic backgrounds would report more parental monitoring, supportiveness, and psychological autonomy than their counterparts from single-mother families and low socioeconomic backgrounds. The hypothesis was supported by the data in the present study. It was found that children from intact families reported more parental monitoring, supportiveness, and psychological autonomy than children from single-mother families. It was also found that children from families with high SES reported having more parental monitoring, supportiveness, and psychological autonomy than children from families with low SES.

These findings echo those of previous studies (Amato, 1987; Astone & McLanahan, 1991; Dornbusch, et al., 1985; Revicki, 1981). Amato (1987) found that adolescents in one-parent families reported that their mothers exercised a relatively low level of control. Astone and McLanahan (1991) also found that children who lived with single parents or stepparents during adolescence received less encouragement and less help with school than children who lived with both natural parents. In addition, Dornbusch and his colleagues (1985) found that adolescents in single-parent families were more likely to make decisions without direct parental input than were children from intact families. As for the relationship between SES and parental practices, Revicki (1981) found that SES and number of siblings correlated with parent involvement in their children's education.

Parental practices are not independent of family status attributes, such as family structure and SES. But why do parental practices vary by family structure and SES? Astone and McLanahan (1991) proposed several hypotheses to explain why parental practices vary by family structure: First, economic resources are generally limited and unreliable in non-intact families. As a result, parents in non-intact families may lower their expectations for children's long-term educational attainment. Second, single-parent as compared to two-parent families had less time and energy to spend on supervising their children. Astone and McLanahan (1991) cited a study by Douthitt to show that single mothers work longer hours outside the home than married mothers. Finally, the parental authority structure may be weaker in single-parent families, partly because single mothers often make confidants of their children. Not all these hypotheses have the same degree of empirical support. Based on the National Survey of Families and Household data, Acock and Demo (1994) found that parenting values reported by mothers did not vary by family type. They argued that family values, rules, and expectations for children could not be determined from family type. Their findings contradicted Astone and McLanahan's first hypothesis. Based on the same data, however, they did find that mothers from intact families reported significantly higher involvement in various school-related, religious, community, and sports activities than did the single mothers. They found that mothers from intact families spent twice as much time as single mothers on school-related activities. Their findings supported the second hypothesis put forward by Astone and McLanahan (1991).

To the question of why parental practices vary by SES, Lareau (1987) suggested that the answer lay in the differences in "cultural capital." In her qualitative study, she found that social class provided parents with unequal quantities of "cultural capital" to comply with teachers' requests for parental participation in school related activities. Working-class parents had fewer economic resources and time to spend on child care and transportation to meet teachers' requests for parental participation. Her claim was consistent with the finding of Revicki (1981) that SES and number of siblings correlated with parent involvement in school. In his study, the higher the SES and the smaller the family, the more active were the parents in classroom volunteering and attendance at meetings and school activities. Dauber and Epstein (1989) also found similar results in their study of 2,317 parents of elementary and middle school students. They found that parents who were better educated and who did not work outside the home were more likely to participate in school activities.

Direct and Indirect Effects of Family Structure and SES on Children's Academic Achievement

Since children's developmental outcomes vary by family processes, and family processes in turn vary by family status, meaningful understanding can only come if we can disentangle the direct and indirect effects of family status on children's development outcomes. There is also a need to determine how family processes mediate the effects of family status on children's development.

Based on the results of path analysis, it was estimated that 16.5% of the total effects of family structure on children's academic achievement were indirect effects via authoritative parenting. Similarly, it was estimated that 28.8% of the total effects of SES on children's academic achievement were indirect effects via authoritative parenting. Authoritative parenting accounted for a significant part of the effects of SES and family structure on children's academic achievement. However, it is noteworthy that the percentage was considerably small. A larger portion, over 70%, of the effects of family structure and SES on children's academic achievement were not mediated by authoritative parenting. This finding is consistent with the findings of Astone and McLanahan's study (1991). In their study, they found that family structure effects were reduced by no more than 15% when parental practices were controlled.

The Effects of Authoritative Parenting on Children's Academic Achievement

In the present study, it was found that parental monitoring and children's academic achievement were significantly correlated. However, 52% of the association was due to the effects of family structure and SES. The causal effects between parental monitoring and children's achievement were reduced to 48% of the total association when the effects of family structure and SES were partialled out. Similarly the causal effects of parental supportiveness and psychological autonomy were reduced to 29.7% and 33.2% respectively of the total association, when the effects of family structure and SES were partialled out. It is noteworthy that family structure and SES accounted for a large portion of the total association between authoritative parenting and children's academic achievement. In contrast, authoritative parenting mediated only a small portion of the total effects of family structure and SES on children's academic achievement.

The Effects of Family Structure and SES on Authoritative Parenting

When the effects of SES were partialled out, the total effects of family structure on the three dimensions of authoritative parenting were drastically reduced. The total effects of family structure on parental monitoring, parental supportiveness and psychological autonomy were reduced to 53.8%, 46.9% and 40.7% respectively, of the total association when the effects of SES were partialled out. In other words, SES accounted for half or more than half of the association between family structure and the three dimensions of authoritative parenting. An opposite pattern emerged when the effects of family structure were partialled out in the association between SES and authoritative parenting. Family structure did not account for a very large portion of the total association between SES and the authoritative parenting. The total effects of SES on parental monitoring, parental supportiveness, and psychological autonomy constituted 84.8%, 85.0%, and 90.7% respectively, of the total association, when the effects of family structure were partialled out. In other words, family structure accounted for only 15% or less of the total association between SES and the three dimensions of authoritative parenting. The contrasting patterns indicate that SES accounts for a major portion of the effects of family structure on authoritative parenting but family structure only accounts for a small portion of the effects of SES on authoritative parenting. This finding substantiates Herzog and Sudia's emphasis (1973) on the importance of controlling for SES in research dealing with the effects of father absence. It also corroborated the findings of previous studies (Acock & Kiecolt, 1989; Milne, et al., 1986; Mueller & Cooper, 1986) that the effects of family structure were minimized after the economic conditions of the families were controlled. This information suggests that parental practice differences in families with different structures are probably related to the socioeconomic conditions of these families

Summary of the Path Analysis

Compared to the social address and the family process paradigms, the integrated paradigm makes it possible to investigate the complicated relationship between family status and family process variables and their interactive influences on the developmental outcomes of children. The results of the path analysis suggested that a small portion of the effects of family structure and SES on children's academic achievement was mediated by authoritative parenting. About 83.5% of the total effects of family structure and 71.2% of the total effects of SES on children's academic achievement were direct effects which were not mediated by authoritative parenting. However, from 52% to 70.3% of the total association between the three dimensions of authoritative parenting and children's academic achievement were due to the effects of family structure and SES. In short, authoritative parenting mediated a small portion of the effects of family structure and SES on children's academic achievement but family structure and SES accounted for a considerably larger portion of the effects of authoritative parenting on children's academic achievement. It was found that authoritative parenting varied by family structure and SES. However, it is noteworthy that from 46.2% to 59.3% of the total association between family structure and the three dimensions of authoritative parenting were due to SES. In contrast, only 9.3% to 15.2% of the total association between SES and the three dimensions of authoritative parenting were due to family structure. This suggests that the lack of economic resources in single-mother families is related to the relatively lower level of authoritative parenting in these families.

It is obvious that the path analysis revealed several significant aspects of the complicated relationships between the social address and family process variables and their interactive effects on children's academic achievement. The results highlight the importance of including both family status and family process variables in the investigation of family influences on children. Ignoring either set of variables results in a myopic view that distorts reality and leads one to ignore pertinent information. An integrative perspective is not only important for researchers, but also for parents, educators, and policy makers who try to draw practical implications from research results, as we will see in the following chapter.

LIMITATIONS AND STRENGTHS OF THE STUDY

Limitations

The two family status variables and the three family process variables in this study accounted for 33.8% of the total variance of the children's GPAs. About 66.2% of the total variance of the children's GPAs were left unexplained. In other words, the children's GPAs were not only affected by the five specified variables but also by many other unspecified variables. Family structure, SES, and the three dimensions of authoritative parenting are by no means the only factors that influences children's academic achievement. Despite the fact that these factors are important factors in children's academic achievement, researchers should also explore other factors that are related to children's academic achievement.

Ethnicity and gender are two important factors related to children's academic achievement that were not included in the present study. As discussed in Chapter II, ethnicity and gender of adolescents has interactive relationships with family structure and parenting style. Baumrind (1991) reminds us that socialization methods which by middle-class white standards appear authoritarian may have utility in preparing African-American adolescents to cope with the hazards of contemporary ghetto life. In the present study, 35.4% of the subjects were

African Americans (see Table 4). Similarly, Zimiles and Lee (1991) found striking gender differences in drop-out behavior in their study of family types and educational outcomes. Children who lived in single-parent families were more likely to drop out when they had an unlike-gender custodial parent. In the present study, 54% of the subjects were from single-mother families (see Table 4). However, gender was not included in the analysis. In order to include ethnicity and gender variables in the analysis, a larger sample size than the present one is needed.

The small sample size places further limits on the present study. The subjects of the study were 181 8th graders from two inner-city schools in the midwestern United States. One can make only limited generalizations from this relatively small sample. Moreover, the data were cross-sectional in nature. Causal relationships in studies with cross-sectional data should be interpreted with caution and prudence. Longitudinal data would allow a more precise evaluation of the effects of the predictive variables. The measures of parenting in this study were obtained by the reports of the children to a questionnaire survey. The lack of other sources of information might have imposed limitations on the accuracy of the measures.

Strengths

In spite of the aforementioned limitations, this study has several strengths. The measures of SES were aggregates of three measures: educational levels of parents, occupational levels of parents, and total family income. In his meta-analysis of previous studies on SES, White (1982) found that measures of SES that combined two or more indicators were more highly correlated with academic achievement than any single indicator (White, 1982). The combination of the three most commonly used SES indicators has enhanced the accuracy of the measures of SES in this study.

The use of actual GPAs instead of self-reported GPAs has also enhanced the accuracy of the measures of children's academic achievement in this study. In most previous studies (Acock & Demo, 1994; Dornbusch, et al. 1987; Lamborn, et al., 1991; Steinberg, et al., 1992), the measures of children's academic achievement were obtained from either parents' reports or children's self-reports. In contrast, the actual GPAs of the children were used in this study as the indicator of academic achievement.

This study did not use the broad categories of two-parent and single-parent families. As reviewed in Chapter II, there are many subtypes of two-parent and single-parent families. Two-parent families and single-parent families are not homogenous groups. Zimiles and Lee (1991) demonstrated that children from subtypes of two-parent families differed in high school grades and educational persistence. In addition, Astone and McLanahan (1991) also demonstrated that there were different parental practices in the subtypes of two-parent families. It is evident that there must be greater differentiation among family types. In this study, the more specific categories of intact and single-mother families were used to replace the broad categories of two-parent and single-parent families.

Another strength of the present study lies in its conceptualization of parenting style. The multi-dimensional approach permits a clear distinction between the subtypes of authoritarian parenting. When the dimension of responsiveness in Baumrind's model is split into two dimensions, supportiveness and psychological autonomy, it is possible to distinguish between the parents who provide firm parental control as well as strong parental support but who grant different levels of psychological autonomy. The new conceptualization of parenting style may resolve the argument about the positive effect of parental control (Lewis, 1981). It may also solve the paradox recently raised by Chao and Sue (1996), who pointed out that in many studies (Dornbusch, et al., 1987; Steinberg, et al., 1992) showed that Asian American parents were non-authoritative while their adolescents had high achievement. There is evidence that Asian American parents provide firm parental control as well as strong parental support to their children (Rohner & Pettengill, 1985). However, it is possible that Asian American parents do not grant much psychological autonomy to their children. If they are high in parental control and supportiveness but low in psychological autonomy, then they are different from the authoritarian parents who are high in parental control but low in supportiveness and psychological autonomy. Different dimensions of authoritative parenting may have different associations with children's developmental outcomes. It is possible that the combination of high parental control and supportiveness is still associated with high academic achievement, even when psychological autonomy is low. Low psychological autonomy may be associated more with children's social-emotional adjustment than with academic achievement. This hypothesis has yet to be subjected to empirical investigation. But it does provide a possible solution to the paradox concerning the association between non-authoritative parenting and high achievement.

The merit of employing an integrated paradigm in the study of family influences is well illustrated in this study. The same set of data was first examined in the social address paradigm, then in the family process paradigm, and finally in the integrated paradigm. Compared to the first two paradigms, the integrated paradigm can better grasp the intricate interaction between family status and family process variables and demonstrate how they interactively influence children's academic achievement. A better understanding of the phenomenon is of paramount importance when we try to translate knowledge into action. In the next chapter, the practical implications of the results are discussed.

VI

Implications

This chapter deals with the practical significance of the present results. In the first section, new directions for future research on the relationships between family factors and children's developmental outcomes are described. In the second section, the implications of the present results for parents, educators, and policy makers are discussed.

DIRECTIONS FOR FUTURE RESEARCH

The present study has demonstrated that the use of an integrated paradigm is justified in research on family factors and children's developmental outcomes. As pointed out by Bronfenbrenner and Crouter (1983), the social address paradigm has one serious limitation: It does not give explicit consideration to intervening process through which the social address might affect the development of children. Compared to the social address paradigm, the family process paradigm does give explicit consideration to the intervening processes that directly affect the developmental outcomes of children. However, a complete shift from the study of social address to the study of family process falls short of the intricate interactions between family status and family processes and how they jointly affect a child's scholastic development. Family status and family processes are not independent or unrelated. It is shown in the study that the three dimensions of authoritative parenting varied by family structure and SES. Children from intact families and high socioeconomic background reported having more parental monitoring, parental supportiveness, and psychological autonomy than children from single-mother families and low socioeconomic background. Family structure and SES accounted for 52% to 70% of the total association between the three dimensions of authoritative parenting and children's academic achievement. On the other hand, the three dimensions of authoritative parenting only mediated 16.5% to 28.8% of the total effects of family structure and SES on children's academic achievement. This offers strong evidence that social address variables have both direct and indirect effects on children, and furthermore, that they should be included in future research on family influences on children. The integrated paradigm that incorporates both social address and family process paradigms can help us achieve a better understanding of the interdependent nature of family status and process factors.

In the present study, the family status variables were socioeconomic status and family structure; the family process variables were the three dimensions of authoritative parenting style; and the outcome variable was the children's academic achievement. Actually, a model that incorporates both family status and process variables can have numerous variations. There are potentially numerous interactive and joint effects of other family status and process variables on other measurable behaviors of children. For example, it may be instructive to use a variant of the present model to conceptualize the relationships between ethnicity, parental involvement in education, and student alienation in school (see figure 11).

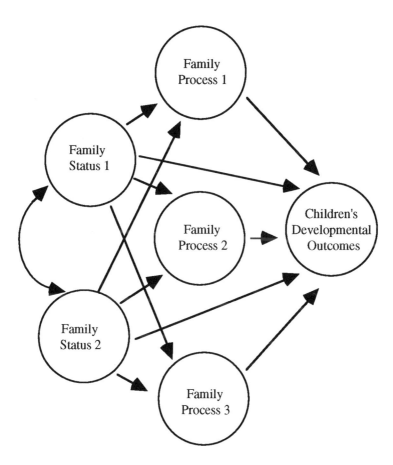

Figure 11. General model incorporating both status and process variables in studies of family effects on children.

The multi-dimensional approach to parenting styles has many advantages over the categorical and two-dimensional approaches. The categorical approach specifies three parenting styles: authoritative, authoritarian, and permissive. However, it does not permit distinctions between indulgent permissive and neglecting parenting styles. The two dimensional approach overcomes this limitation by a fourfold classification of parenting styles. With the combination of different levels of the two dimensions of demandingness and responsiveness, four parenting styles can be identified: authoritative, authoritarian, permissive, and neglecting/ignoring.

Parents who are low in both demandingness and responsiveness are identified as neglecting or ignoring. However, the two dimensional approach itself is susceptible to confusion. Lewis (1981) challenged the positive effect of high parental control as she perceived autonomy or the democratic element being precluded in high parental control. However, autonomy or a democratic element is present in authoritative parenting and is embedded in the dimension of responsiveness. To avoid confusion, it is better to split the responsiveness dimensions into two components: Parental supportiveness and psychological autonomy.

With a multi-dimensional approach to parenting, finer distinctions among the different parenting styles are possible. Conceptually, there can be eight parenting styles according to the combination of different levels of the three dimensions (see Table 12). Not all the eight parenting styles in Table 22 are empirically meaningful although all are theoretically possible. However, some of them deserve further exploration. For example, subtypes 1 and 2 of authoritarian parenting are especially relevant to the present discussion. The distinction between these two subtypes may resolve the paradox raised by Chao and Sue (1996) about the parenting style of Asian

American parents. However, these speculations have not as yet been empirically substantiated. More research is needed to test the effects of these authoritarian parenting subtypes.

Table 22
Eight Possible Parenting Styles

Parenting Style	Parental Monitoring	Parental Supportiveness	Psychological Autonomy
Authoritative	High	High	High
Authoritarian (subtype 1)	High	High	Low
Authoritarian (subtype 2)	High	Low	Low
Authoritarian (subtype 3)	High	Low	High
Permissive (subtype 1)	Low	High	High
Permissive (subtype 2)	Low	High	Low
Permissive (subtype 3)	Low	Low	High
Rejecting/ Neglecting	Low	Low	Low

IMPLICATIONS FOR PARENTS AND EDUCATORS

Authoritative parenting is consistently found to be associated with better developmental outcomes of children. Such effective parenting includes (1) a high degree of monitoring, (2) a high degree of support or involvement, and (3) a high degree of psychological autonomy-granting. However, parenting with all these elements does not seem to be prevalent. In a just-completed survey of 20,000 families of adolescents from various socioeconomic backgrounds, Steinberg (cited in Sandmaier, 1996), found that 25% of parents seldom talked with their adolescents about the day's events, were not sure how they spent time and seldom did anything with them for fun. In an in-depth study of 55 mother-father-young adolescents triads in Chicago area, Larson and Richards (1994) found that mothers, fathers, and young adolescents spent respectively 12.1%, 5.8% and 5.9% of their time on family talk. In comparison, they spent respectively 11.6%, 13.2% and 15.0% of their time on media. It is noteworthy that fathers and young adolescents spent more time on media than on family talk.

The fact that parental practices vary by family structure and SES indicates that conditions favoring authoritative parenting may also vary by family structure and SES. As discussed in the previous chapter, single parents as compared to parents from two-parent families may have less time and energy to spend on supervising their children. In addition, parents of low SES may have less "cultural capital" to comply with teachers' requests for parental participation in school. Huang and Gibbs (1992) have critically claimed that schools, for the most part, are middle-class institutions, as reflected in the attitudes of their personnel. As a result, there are often value, attitude, and behavioral differences between parents and educators. To foster more involvement and participation in school activities by parents of various family types and socioeconomic backgrounds, educators need to be sensitive to their customary practices. For example, conferences should be scheduled so that both working parents, and single parents can attend. School personnel should also consider providing child care for younger children during parent-teacher conferences. In her handbook on families, Cline (1990) suggests that schools should also consider charging fees on a sliding scale when they arrange events and special trips for single parents with limited incomes. She also suggests that school teachers and administrators should be more sensitive to single-parent or divorce situations when they communicate with students' families. Newsletters and notes are better addressed to "parent/guardian" or "family" instead of "mom" or "dad." School personnel should also allow students to bring either parent or even an unrelated but special adult to school events.

IMPLICATION FOR POLICY MAKERS

Educators are not the only people who can help parents remove hurdles to effective parenting. Policy makers have an important role to play in this respect. Ruth Sidel a professor of sociology at the City University of New York argues (1992) that funding social programs would benefit families. As indicated in the present study, half or over half of the total association between family structure and authoritative parenting is due to the effects of SES. The lack of economic resources in single-mother families is related to the relatively low level of authoritative parenting in these families. To promote effective parenting in all families, the government first needs to address the phenomenon of "feminization of poverty." As discussed in Chapter I, a considerable number of single-mother families in the U.S. are living below the poverty line. The causes for this phenomenon are numerous. Sidel (1992) argues that a key factor in the pauperization of women is the existence of a dual labor market that discriminates against female workers. She states that working women on average earn only 68 cents on every dollar that men earn. She advocates reform in the work arena that ends economic discrimination against women.

I agree with Sidel that ending discrimination against women in employment is important. However, I also believe that it is equally important to help single mothers to develop marketable skills. Education for some single mothers might have been disrupted if they became pregnant while they were still in school. Lack of marketable skills and child care support may keep single mothers on welfare. Pilot (1987) reported that the overwhelming majority of teenage mothers interviewed in a survey said that they would rather work than be on welfare. However, they indicated that they needed help in developing marketable skills. Social programs that help single mothers complete high school diplomas and receive vocational training will enable these women to achieve financial independence for themselves and their children. In addition, affordable day care and after school care for children are needed to help those single working mothers who struggle to balance their career and family responsibilities. Last but not least, state governments and courts should be more rigorous in requiring and procuring child support from non-custodian fathers. Child support payments will definitely help single mothers who are struggling financially to support their families.

CONCLUSIONS

How the family influences children's academic achievement is the main concern of the present study. Instead of focusing on either family status or family processes, the study examines both sets of variables and their interactive effect on children's academic achievement. The results of the study indicates that the integrated research paradigm can help researchers better understand the intricate relations among various family factors and their impact on children. The effort to promote positive family processes will not be successful unless we recognize the intricate linkage between family status and family processes. The integrated research paradigm enables us to understand the need to promote desirable conditions and remove undesirable ones in the social environment that undermine positive family processes. This understanding is important for parents, educators and policy makers in their mutual concern for the well being of children.

Appendix A

Name: _____
I.D.: _____
School: _____
Grade: _____

── Parent-Child Interaction Questionnaire ──

Who are the people you are living with? (check all that apply)
❏ Mother ❏ Father ❏ Step-mother ❏ Step-father
❏ Grandparents ❏ Foster Parents ❏ Brothers/Sisters ❏ Other

Please answer the following questions in reference to the parent(s) with whom you are living:

1. In a typical week, what is the latest you can stay out on SCHOOL NIGHTS (Sunday-Thursday)?
   (Circle one choice)
   1. not allowed out after school
   2. depends on circumstances but approved by my parent(s)
   3. before 8:00
   4. before 10:00
   5. as late as I want

2. In a typical week, what is the latest you can stay out on FRIDAY or SATURDAY NIGHTS?
   (Circle one choice)
   1. not allowed out
   2. depends on cirucmstances but approved by my parent(s)
   3. before 9:00
   4. before 11:00
   5. as late as I want

	Very much	Pretty much	Somewhat	Not much	Not at all
3. How much do your parent(s) TRY to know about . . .					
• where you go at night?	1	2	3	4	5
• what you do with your free time?	1	2	3	4	5
• where you are most afternoons after school?	1	2	3	4	5
4. How much do your parent(s) REALLY know about . . .					
• where you go at night?	1	2	3	4	5
• what you do with your free time?	1	2	3	4	5
• where you are most afternoons after school?	1	2	3	4	5
5. How much do your parent(s) really know who your friends are?	1	2	3	4	5

	Almost everyday	A few times a week	month	year	Almost never
6. How often do these things happen in your family?					
• My parent(s) spend time just talking with me.	1	2	3	4	5
• My family does something fun together.	1	2	3	4	5

	Almost always	Often	Sometimes	Rarely	Almost never
7. When you get a poor grade (D or below), how often do you get the following reactions from your parent(s)? (Circle one choice for each line)					
• They get upset with me.	1	2	3	4	5
• They encourage me to try harder.	1	2	3	4	5
• I am grounded.	1	2	3	4	5
• They offer to help me.	1	2	3	4	5
8. When you get a good grade (A or B), how often do you get the following reaction from your parent(s)? (Circle one choice for each line)					
• They praise me.	1	2	3	4	5
• They tell me that I should do even better.	1	2	3	4	5
• They tell me that my other grades should be better.	1	2	3	4	5

Page 1 of 2

107

9. How often are the following statements true about your parent(s):

	Almost always	Often	Sometimes	Rarely	Almost never
• They will not let me do things with them when I do something they don't like.	1	2	3	4	5
• They let me make my own plans for things I want to do.	1	2	3	4	5
• They will act cold and unfriendly if I do something they do not like.	1	2	3	4	5
• They help me with schoolwork if there is something I do not understand.	1	2	3	4	5
• When they want me to do something, they explain why.	1	2	3	4	5
• I can count on them to help me out, if I have some kind of problems.	1	2	3	4	5

10. These are some of the things that parents say to their children. Please indicate for each of the following items how often you hear similar things:

	Almost always	Often	Sometimes	Rarely	Almost never
• They tell you that their ideas are correct and that you should not question them.	1	2	3	4	5
• They answer your arguments by saying something like "You'll know better when you grow up".	1	2	3	4	5
• They admit that children know more about some things than adults do.	1	2	3	4	5
• We talk at home about things like politics or religion, where one person may take a different side from others.	1	2	3	4	5

11. Please indicate how much your parent(s) emphasize the following things:
Do they emphasize . . .

	Very much	Pretty much	Somewhat	Not much	Not at all
• that every member of your family should have some say in family decisions?	1	2	3	4	5
• that you should not argue with adults?	1	2	3	4	5

	Almost always	Often	Sometimes	Rarely	Almost never
12. My parent(s) supervise and monitor me closely.	1	2	3	4	5
13. My parent(s) are caring, supportive and involved.	1	2	3	4	5
14. My parent(s) encourage me to express my individuality and consider my opinions in making decisions that affect me.	1	2	3	4	5

Adapted from the questionnaires by Dornbusch, S.M, et al. (1987) and Steinberg, L., et al. (1991)   Page 2 of 2

Appendix B

Scoring Scheme of the Parent-Child Interaction Questionnaire

Parental Monitoring (MON)

Number of Responses: 8   Range of Scores: 8 - 40

1. In a typical week, what is the latest you can stay out on SCHOOL NIGHTS (Monday-Thursday)? ["not allowed out", "depends on circumstances but approved by my parents", "before 8:00", "before 10:00", "as late as I want"] (Adapted from Steinberg et al., 1991)

2. In a typical week, what is the latest you can stay out on FRIDAY OR SATURDAY NIGHT? ["not allowed out", "depends on circumstances but approved by my parents", "before 9:00", "before 11:00", "as late as I want"] (Adapted from Steinberg et al., 1991)

3. How much do your parents TRY to know . . . ["very much", "pretty much", "somewhat", "not much", "not at all"]
    - Where you go at night?
    - What you do with your free time?
    - Where you are most afternoons after school?
   (Adapted from Steinberg et al., 1991)

4. How much do your parents REALLY know . . . ["very much", "pretty much", "somewhat", "not much", "not at all"]
    - Where you go at night?
    - What you do with your free time?
    - Where you are most afternoons after school?
   (Adapted from Steinberg et al., 1991)

Parental Supportiveness (SUP)

Number of Responses: 12   Range of Scores: 12 - 60

5. How much do your parents REALLY know who your friends
   are? ["very much", "pretty much", "somewhat", "not much",
   "not at all"]
   (Adapted from Steinberg et al., 1991)

6. How often do these things happen in your family? ["almost
   everyday', "a few times a week", "a few times a month", "a
   few times a year", "almost never"]
       - My parents spend time just talking with me.
       - My family does something fun together.
   (Adapted from Steinberg et al., 1991)

7. When you get a POOR grade, how often do you get the
   following reactions from your parents? ["almost always",
   "often", "sometimes", "rarely", "almost never"]
       *- They get upset with me.
       - They encourage me to try harder
       - They offer to help me
       *- I am grounded
   (Adapted from Dornbusch et al., 1987)

8. When you get a GOOD grade, how often do you get the
   following reactions from your parents? ["almost always",
   "often", "sometimes", "rarely", "almost never"]
       - They praise me
       *- They tell me that I should do even better
       *- They tell me that my other grades should be better
   (Adapted from Dornbusch et al., 1987)

9. How often are the following statements true about your
   parents: ["almost always", "often", "sometimes", "rarely",
   "never"]

- They help me with my schoolwork if there is
something I don't understand.
- I can count on them to help me out if I have some kind
of problem.
(Adapted from Steinberg et al., 1991)

Psychological Autonomy (AUT)
Number of Responses: 10   Range of Scores: 10 - 50

9. How often are the following statements true about your
parents: ["almost always", "often", "sometimes", "rarely",
"never"]
    *- They won't let me do things with them when I do
something they don't like.
    - They let me make my own plans for things I want to
do.
    *- They act cold and unfriendly if I do something they
don't like.
    - When they want me to do something, they explains
why.
    (Adapted from Steinberg et al., 1991)

10. These are some of the things that parents say to their
children. Please think about your family conversations and
indicate for each of the following items how often you hear
similar things: ["almost always", "often", "sometimes",
"rarely", "never"]
Do they
    *- tell you that parents' ideas are correct and that
children should not
question them.
    *- answer your arguments by saying 'you'll know better
when you grow
up'.

  - admit that children know more about some things
    than adults do.
  - that every member of the family should have say in
    family decisions.
  - talk at home about things like politics or religion,
    where one takes a
    different side from others.
(Adapted from Dornbusch et al., 1987)

11. Please indicate how much your parents emphasize the
    following things: ["very much", "pretty much",
    "somewhat", "Not much", "not at all"]
      - that every member of the family should have some
        say in family
        decisions.
      *- that you shouldn't argue with adults.
    (Adapted from Dornbusch et al., 1987)

Note. The items with an * score 1 for the first response, 2 for second, 3
for third, 4 for fourth, and 5 for the fifth. The contrary will be true for
the items without an *. They score 5 for the first response, 4 for second, 3
for third, 2 for fourth, and 1 for the fifth.

Appendix C

Demographic Data

Student _____
I.D.   _____
School _____

1. Occupation of the parents   Duncan Socioeconomic Index
Mother_____   _____
Father_____   _____
Family   _____

2. Education level of mother
- ❑ Less than 7th grade
- ❑ 7th to 8th grade
- ❑ 9th grade
- ❑ 10th to 11th grade
- ❑ High school graduate (12 grade)
- ❑ Some college
- ❑ College graduate
- ❑ Graduate School

3. Education level of father
- ❑ Less than 7th grade
- ❑ 7th to 8th grade
- ❑ 9th grade
- ❑ 10th to 11th grade
- ❑ High school graduate (12 grade)
- ❑ Some college
- ❑ College graduate
- ❑ Graduate School

4. Total family income before taxes in 1992_____

References

Acock, A. C. & Demo, D. H. (1994). *Family diversity and well being.* Thousand Oaks, CA: Sage Publications.

Acock, A. C. & Kiecolt, K. J. (1989). Is it family structure or socioeconomic status? Family structure during adolescence and adult adjustment. *Social Forces, 68*(2), 553-571.

Alwin, D. & Hauser, R. M. (1975). The decomposition of effects in path analysis. *American Sociological Review, 40,* 37-47.

Amato, P. R. (1987). Family processes in one-parent, stepparent, and intact families: The child's point of view. *Journal of Marriage and the Family, 49*(2), 327-337.

Amato, P. R. & Keith, B. (1991). parental divorce and the well-being of children: A meta-analysis. *Psychological Bulletin, 110*(1), 26-46.

Amber, A., & Saucier, J. (1984). Adolescents' academic success and aspirations by parental marital status. *Canadian Review of Sociology and Anthropology, 21*(1), 62-71.

Astone, N. M., & McLanahan, S. S. (1991). Family structure, parental practices and high school completion. *American Sociological Review, 56,* 309-320.

Baron, R. M. & Kenny, D. A. (1986). The moderator-mediator variable distinction in social psychological research: Conceptual, strategic, and statistical considerations. *Journal of Personality and Social Psychology, 51*(6), 1173-1182.

Baumrind, D. (1967). Child care practices anteceding three patterns of preschool behavior. *Genetic Psychology Monographs, 75,* 43-88.

Baumrind, D. (1971). Current patterns of parental authority. *Developmental Psychology Monograph, 4*(1, Pt.2).

Baumrind, D. (1977). *Socialization determinants of personal agency.* Paper presented at the meeting of the Society for Research in Child Development, New Orleans, March 27-30.

Baumrind, D. (1979). *Sex-related socialization effects.* Paper presented at the meeting of the Society for Research in Child Development, San Francisco.

Baumrind, D. (1989). Rearing competent children. In W. Damon (Ed.), *Child development today and tomorrow* (pp.349-378). San Francisco: Jossey-Bass.

Baumrind, D. (1991). Parenting styles and adolescent development. In J. Brooks-Gunn, R. Lerner, A. C. Peterson (Eds.), *The encyclopedia of adolescence.* New York: Garland.

Becker, W. C. (1964). Consequences of different kinds of parental discipline. In M. L. Hoffman & L. W. Hoffman (Eds.), *Review of child development research. Vol. 1.* New York: Russell Sage Foundation.

Blum, H. M., Boyle, M. H., & Offord, D. R. (1988). Single-parent families: child psychiatric disorder and school performance. *Journal of the American Academy of Child and Adolescent Psychiatry, 27*(2), 214-219.

Blau P. M. & Duncan, O. D. (1967) *The American occupational structure.* New York: Wiley.

British Psychological Society. (1986). Achievement in the primary school: Evidence to the Education, Science and Arts Committee of the House of Commons. *Bulletin of the British Pscyhological Society, 39,* 121-125.

Bronfenbrenner, U., & Crouter, A. C. (1983). The evolution of environmental models in developmental research. In E. M. Hetherington (Ed.), P. H. Musen (Series Ed.), *Handbook of child psychology: Vol. 1. Socialization, personality and social development* (pp.357-414). New York: Wiley.

Christenson, S. L., Rounds, T., & Gorney, D. (1992). Family factors and student achievement: An avenue to increase students' success. *School Psychology Quarterly, 7*(3), 178-206.

Chao, R. & Sue, S. (1996). Chinese parental influence and their children's school success: A paradox in the literature on parenting styles. In S. Lau (Ed.), *Growing up the Chinese way* (pp.93-120). Hong Kong: Chinese University Press.

Clark, R. (1983). *Family life and school achievement: Why poor black children succeed or fail.* Chicago: University of Chicago Press.

Cline, R. (1990). *Focus on families.* Santa Barbara, CA: ABC-CLIO.

Coleman, J., Campbell, E. Q., Hobson, C. J., McPartland, J., Mood, A. M., Weinfeld, F. D., & York, R. L. (1966). *Equality of educational opportunity survey* (A publication of the National Center for Educational Statistics). Washington, D. C.: U.S. Government Printing Office.

Collins. W. A. (1990). Parent-child relationships in the transition to adolescence: Continuity and change in interaction, affect, and cognition. In R. Montemayor, G.R. Adams, & T.P. Gullotta (Eds.), *Advances in adolescent development: An annual book series: Vol. 2. From childhood to adolescence: A transitional period?* (pp.85-106) Newbury Park, CA:Sage.

Datcher-Loury, L. (1988). Family background and school achievement among low income Blacks. *The Journal of Human Resources, 24*(3), 528-544.

Dauber, S. L, & Epstein, J. L. (1989, April) *Parent attitudes and practices of involvement in inner-city elementary and middle schools.* Paper presented at the annual meeting of American Educational Research Association, San Francisco.

Dornbusch, S. M., Carlsmith, S. J., Bushwall, S. J., Ritter, P. L., Leiderman, H., Hastorf, A. H. & Gross, R. T. (1985). Single parents, extended households, and the control of adolescents. *Child Development, 56,* 326-341.

Dornbusch, S. M., Ritter, P. L., Leiderman, P. H., Roberts, D. F., & Fraleigh, M. J. (1987). The relation of parenting style to adolescent school performance. *Child Development, 58,* 1244-1257.

Dornbusch, S. M. & Wood, K. D. (1989). Family processes and educational achievement. In W. J. Weston (Ed.), *Education and the American family - A research syntheses.* (pp.66-95) New York: New York University Press.

Eagle, E. (1989). *Socioeconomic status, family structure, and parental involvement: the correlates of achievement.* (ERIC Document Reproduction Service. No. ED307 332).

Featherstone, D. R. Cundick, B. P. & Jensen, L. C. (1992). Differences in school behavior and achievement between children from intact, reconstituted, and single-parent families. *Adolescence, 27*(106), 1-12.

Flanangan, J. C., Shaycroft, M. F., Richards, J. M., & Claudy, G. J. (1971). *Five years after high school.* Palo Alto, Calif: American Institutes for Research.

Grolnick, W. S. & Ryan, R. M. (1989). Parent styles associated with children's self-regulation and competence in school. *Journal of Educational Psychology, 81*(2), 143-154.

Halsey, A. H. (1975). Sociology and the equality debate. *Oxford Review of Education, 1*, 9-23.

Health, P. A. & MacKinnon, C. (1988). Factors related to the social competence of children in single-parent families. *Journal of Divorce, 11*(3/4), 49-66.

Herzog, E. & Sudia, C. (1973). Children in fatherless families. In B. V. Caldwell & H. N. Ricuiti (Eds.), *Review of child development research: Vol. 3. Child development and child policy.* Chicago: University of Chicago Press.

Hetherington, E. M. (1992). Coping with marital transitions: A family systems perspective. *Monographs of the Society for Research in Child Development, 57* (2-3), 1-34.

Huang, L. N. & Gibbs, J. T. (1992). Partners or adversaries? Home-school collaboration across culture, race, and identity. In S. L. Christenson & J. C. Conoley (Eds.), *Home-school collaboration: Enhancing children's academic and social competence* (pp.81-109). Silver Spring, MD: NASP.

Kohn, M. L. (1977). *Class and conformity: A study in values.* Chicago: The University of Chicago Press.

Kohn, M. L. (1979). The effects of social class on parental values and practices. In H. A. Hoffman (Ed.), *The American family: Dying or developing.* New York: Plenum Press.

Lamborn, S. D., Mounts, N. S., Steinberg, L., & Dornbusch, S. M. (1991). Patterns of competence and adjustment among adolescents from authoritative, authoritarian, indulgent and neglectful families. *Child Development, 62*(5), 1049-1065.

Lareau, A. (1987). Social class differences in family-school relationships: The importance of cultural capital. *Sociology of Education, 60,* 73-85.

Larson, R. & Richards, M. H. (1994). *Divergent realities: The emotional lives of mothers, fathers, and adolescents.* New York: Basic Book.

Lewis, C. (1981). The effects of parental firm control: A reinterpretation of findings. *Psychological Bulletin, 90,* 547-563.

Maccoby, E., & Martin, J. (1983). Socialization in the context of the family: Parent-child interaction. In E. M. Hetherington (Ed.), P. H. Musen (Series Ed.), *Handbook of child psychology: Vol. 4. Socialization, personality and social development* (pp.1-101). New York: Wiley.

Marjoribanks, K. (1980). *Ethnic families and children's achievements.* Sydney: Allen & Unwin.

Marjoribanks, K. (1988). Perceptions of family environments, educational and occupational outcomes: Social-status differences. *Perceptual and Motor Skills, 66,* 3-9.

Milne, A.M. (1989). Family structure and the Achievement of children. In W. J. Weston (Ed.), *Education and the American family - A research syntheses* (pp.32-65). New York: New York University Press.

Milne, A. M., Myers, D. E., Rosenthal, A.S., & Ginsburg, A. (1986). Single parents, working mothers, and the educational achievement of school children. *Sociology of Education, 59,* 125-139.

Mueller, C.W. & Parcel, T.L. (1981). Measures of socioeconomic status: Alternatives and recommendations. *Child Development, 52,* 13-30.

Mueller, D. P. & Cooper, P. W. (1986). Children of single parent families: How they fare as young adults. *Family Relations, 35,* 169-176.

Orthner, D.K. & Pittman, J.F. (1986). Family contributions to work commitment. *Journal of Marriage and the Family, 48,* 573-581.

Patterson, C. J., Kupersmidt, J. B., & Vaden, N. A. (1990). Income level, gender, ethnicity, and household composition as predictors of children's school-based competence. *Child Development, 61,* 485-494.

Patterson, G. R. & Stouthamer-Loeber, M. (1984). The correlation of family management practices and delinquency. *Child Development, 55,* 1299-1307.

Paulson, S. E. (1992). *Adolesncents' and their parents' perceptions of parenting styles: Relations with achievement.* (ERIC Document Reproduction Service. No. ED 351 139).

Paulson, S.E., Hill, J.P., & Holmbeck, G.N. (1991). Distinguishing between perceived closeness and parental warmth in families with seventh-grade boys and girls. *Journal of Early Adolescence, 11,* 276-293.

Pilot, D. F. (1987). Routes to self-sufficiency: Teenage mothers and employment, *Children Today, 16*(1), 6-11.

Revicki, D. A. (1981). *The relationship among socioeconomic status, home environment, parent involvement, child self concept, and child achievement.* (ERIC Document Reproduction Service. No. ED 206 645)

Rohner, R., & Pettengill, S. (1985). Perceived parental acceptance, rejection and parental control among Korean adolescents. *Child Development, 56,* 524-528.

Rutter, M., Tizard, J., & Whitmore, K. (1970). *Education, health, and behavior.* New York: Wiley.

Sandmaier, M. (1996). More than love. *The Family Therapy Networker, 20*(3), 20-33.

Schaefer, E. (1959). A circumplex model for maternal behavior. *Journal of Abnormal and Social Psychology, 59,* 226-235.

Schucksmith, J. Hendry, L. B., Glendinning, A. (1995). Models of parenting: Implications for adolescent well-being within different types of family contexts. *Journal of Adolescence, 18*(3), 253-270.

Sidel, R. (1992). Funding social programs would benefit families. In V. Wagner (Ed.), *The family in America: Opposing viewpoints* (pp.234-241). San Diego, CA: Greenhaven Press.

Steinberg, L. (1990). Interdependency in the family: Autonomy, conflict, and harmony in the parent-adolescent relationship. In S. Feldman & G. Elliot (Eds.), *At the threshold: The developing adolescent.* Cambridge, MA: Harvard University Press.

Steinberg, L., Elmen, J.D., & Mounts, N.S. (1989). Authoritative parenting, psychosocial maturity, and academic success among adolescents. *Child Development, 60,* 1424-1436.

Steinberg, L., Mounts, N. S., Lamborn, S. D., Dornbusch, S. M. (1991). Authoritative parenting and adolescent adjustment across varied ecological niches. *Journal of Research on Adolescence, 1*(1), 19-36.

Steinberg, L., Dornbusch, S. M. & Brown, B. B. (1992). Ethnic differences in adolescent achievement: An ecological perspective. *American Psychologist, 47*(6), 723-729.

Stevens, G. & Cho. J. H. (1985). Socioeconomic Indexes and the new 1980 Census occupational classification scheme. *Social Science Research, 14,* 142-168.

Walters, M. (1988). Single-parent, female headed households. In M. Walters (Ed.), *The invisible web: Gender patterns in family relationships.* New York: Guilford Press.

West, D. J., & Farrington, D. P. (1977). *Who becomes delinquent?* London: Heinenmann.

White, D. R. (1982). The relation between socioeconomic status and academic achievement. *Psychological Bulletin, 9*(3), 461-481.

Wright, D.W. & Price, S.J. (1986). Court-ordered child support payment: The effect of former-spouse relationship on compliance. *Journal of Marriage and the Family, 48,* 867-874.

Zimiles, H. & Lee, V. E. (1991). Adolescent family structure and educational progress. *Development Psychology,* 27(5), 314-320.

Index